First World War
and Army of Occupation
War Diary
France, Belgium and Germany

27 DIVISION
Divisional Troops
Royal Army Medical Corps
83 Field Ambulance
and 7 Sanitary Section
27 December 1914 - 30 November 1915

WO95/2259/3-4

The Naval & Military Press Ltd
www.nmarchive.com
Published in association with The National Archives

Published by

The Naval & Military Press Ltd

Unit 10 Ridgewood Industrial Park,
Uckfield, East Sussex,
TN22 5QE England
Tel: +44 (0) 1825 749494

www.naval-military-press.com

www.nmarchive.com

This diary has been reprinted in facsimile from the original. Any imperfections are inevitably reproduced and the quality may fall short of modern type and cartographic standards.

© Crown Copyright
Images reproduced by permission of The National Archives, London, England, 2015.

Contents

Document type	Place/Title	Date From	Date To
Heading	WO95/2259/3		
Heading	27th Division Medical 83rd Field Ambulance Dec 1914-Nov 1915		
Heading	121/4256 Dec 27th 1914 Jan 27th 1915 83rd Field Ambulance-27th Division Vol I		
War Diary	Blaringham	27/12/1914	27/01/1915
Heading	War Diary from admission and Discharge Book of 83rd Field Ambulance Galdsee Lt Col o/c 83rd Field Ambce Feb 2/15		
Heading	War Diary of 83rd Field Ambulance, R.A.M.C. From 21st April, 1915 To 30th April, 1915 Vol IV		
Miscellaneous			
War Diary	L'Abbe Farm Crombeke Road Nr Poperinghe	21/04/1915	30/04/1915
Heading	27th Division 83rd Field Ambulance Vol V May 1915		
War Diary	L'Abbe Farm Nr Poperinghe	01/05/1915	31/05/1915
War Diary	Locre	31/05/1915	31/05/1915
Heading	27th Division War Diary Of 83rd Field Ambulance, RAMC From 1st June 1915 To 30th June 1915 Vol VI		
War Diary	Locre	01/06/1915	01/06/1915
War Diary	Armentieres	01/06/1915	30/06/1915
Heading	27th Division 121/6292 83rd Field Ambulance Vol VII July 15		
Heading	83rd Field Ambulance RAMC War Diary July, 1915		
War Diary	Armentieres	01/07/1915	18/07/1915
War Diary	Ferme Hollebere Armentieres	19/07/1915	25/07/1915
War Diary	Hollebeque Farm Armentieres	26/07/1915	31/07/1915
Heading	27th Division 83rd Field Ambulance RAMC War Diary August, 1915 Vol VIII		
War Diary	Hollebeque Farm Armentieres	01/08/1915	31/08/1915
Heading	27th Division War Diary Of 83rd Field Ambulance RAMC Vol IX September 1915		
War Diary	Hollebeque Farm Armentieres	01/09/1915	14/09/1915
War Diary	Strazeele	15/09/1915	17/09/1915
War Diary	Thiennes	18/09/1915	18/09/1915
War Diary	Guillaucourt	18/09/1915	18/09/1915
War Diary	Morcourt	19/09/1915	20/09/1915
War Diary	Froissy	20/09/1915	21/09/1915
War Diary	La Neuville Les Bray	22/09/1915	30/09/1915
Heading	27th Division War Diary Of 83rd Field Ambulance RAMC T.F. October, 1915 Vol X		
War Diary	La Neuville L. Bray	01/10/1915	25/10/1915
War Diary	Morcourt	26/10/1915	26/10/1915
War Diary	Boves	27/10/1915	27/10/1915
War Diary	Fluy	28/10/1915	02/11/1915
Heading	27th Div War Diary Of 83rd Field Ambulance, RAMC T.F. November 1915 Vol XI		
War Diary	Fluy	01/11/1915	30/11/1915
Heading	WO95/2259/4		
Heading	27th Division Medical No. 7 Sanitary Section Dec 1915		
Heading	27th Div F/260/1 Dec 1915 7 San Sect		

War Diary	Bovelles France	01/12/1915	03/12/1915
War Diary	Marseilles France	04/12/1915	31/12/1915

WO95/2259/3

27TH DIVISION
MEDICAL

83RD FIELD AMBULANCE
DEC 1914 - NOV 1915

83rd Field Ambulance. — 24th Division

Vol I.

83rd Field Ambulance

WAR DIARY
or
INTELLIGENCE SUMMARY.
(Erase heading not required.)

Army Form C. 2118.

Instructions regarding War Diaries and Intelligence Summaries are contained in F.S. Regs., Part II and the Staff Manual respectively. Title pages will be prepared in manuscript.

Hour, Date, Place	Summary of Events and Information	Remarks and references to Appendices
Blaringhem Dec: 27th 1914:	Yesterday, the 26th Dec, the 83rd Field Ambulance marched from ARQUES relieving 4th BIRMINGHAM, and directs. This (27th) morning we opened a School as a Dressing Station, and received 6 patients; from various Battalions of the 25th Brigade. They were chiefly chill and cold. Seven patients were admitted.	All three cases were attributable to the damp weather and cold winds, affecting troops drawn from India, &c. There were no infectious cases recorded, and as a whole the health of the Brigade was good.
Dec. 28 "	One " " " "	
" 29 "	" " " " "	
" 30 "	Ten " " " "	
" 31 "	Nine " " " "	
Jan? 1. 1915	Twelve " " " "	
" 2 "	Seven " " " "	
" 3 "	Fifteen " " " "	
" 4 "	Rest Station Closed, and preparations made to march to Strazeele. STRAZEELE	
" 5 "	Marched with Brigade to STRAZEELE a distance of about twelve miles. Ten minute halts every hour were made and there were no casualties on the road.	

Army Form C. 2118.

WAR DIARY or INTELLIGENCE SUMMARY.
(Erase heading not required.)

Instructions regarding War Diaries and Intelligence Summaries are contained in F.S. Regs., Part II. and the Staff Manual respectively. Title pages will be prepared in manuscript.

Hour, Date, Place	Summary of Events and Information	Remarks and references to Appendices
Jan. 6. 1915	Left STRAZEELE 9.30 a.m. behind Ammunition Column. Considerable delay was caused by a piebald horse in this column reverting in our losing our position with the first column, and marching in rear of 2nd column, in consequence we reached DICKEBUSCH after dark. Notwithstanding the musketry march was about fifteen miles. Princess Patricia's C. & D. ans King's Royal Rifles went into huts and relieved the French. The weather during the day was fine but rained in evening.	It frequently happens that the Field Ambulance is held up by some transport or breaking down or faulty horse. I would suggest they should provide a vehicle and remain their position in the Column.
Jan. 7. 1915.	Explored country outside DICKEBUSCH, in Brigade Area for Advanced Dressing Station, but no site available. The only one to be had was a school in DICKEBUSCH itself within Rifle fire and consequently too far forward. This place was cleaned and scrubbed down, many traces of dirt shown and after having the cleaned. The clothes were fumigated found and at 3 p.m. the place was ready for the reception of casualties. The ablution and Disinfector was started and at this day was closed at 12 noon. 16 Patients were admitted, including LIEUT. C.W. FINNEMORE of P.P.C.L.I. injury to knees, and sprained

(73989) W.14141—463. 400,000. 9/14. H.&J.Ltd. Forms/C. 2118/10.

Army Form C. 2118.

WAR DIARY
or
INTELLIGENCE SUMMARY.
(Erase heading not required.)

Instructions regarding War Diaries and Intelligence Summaries are contained in F.S. Regts., Part II and the Staff Manual respectively. Title pages will be prepared in manuscript.

Hour, Date, Place	Summary of Events and Information	Remarks and references to Appendices
Jan. 7. 1915 (cont)	from have kick and CAPT. CUTHBERT. SMITH. of P.P.C.L.I.; two Batley of others of the remaining 14, two cases were wounds, and the rest chiefly rheumatism.	wounds. 2
Jan. 8. -	Twenty nine cases were admitted of which 18 were wounds. The remaining being chiefly rheumatism.	wounds. ₤13.
Jan. 9. -	Fifty six cases were admitted of which 24 were wounds. The remainder being chiefly rheumatism. LIEUT. MADDEN of the Argyle & S.H., and CAPT. D.O.C. NEWTON, of P.P.C.L.I. and CAPT. D.O.C. NEWTON, of P.P.C.L.I. and MAJOR. J. W. McKINFREY of P.P.C.L.I. were among the wounded; and MAJOR. J. W. McKINFREY of P.P.C.L.I. has rheumatism.	wounds. 24 The rest rheumatism began to affect the health and physique condition of the men.
Jan. 10. "	158 Cases were admitted on this day, of which 17 were wounds. The remainder being chiefly rheumatism. Of these CAPT. A. R. T. WILSON of the ARGYLE & S. H., and 2ⁿᵈ LIEUT. H. W. MORGAN, and G. EDEN, of 4. K. R. R., were suffering from exposure, with oedema of feet.	wounds. 17 There is further evidence of the effect of the wet weather.
Jan. 11. "	96 Cases were admitted. There were no wounds, and nearly all were suffering from exposure and swollen feet. One case of DYSENTERY and one case of ENTERIC are includes, from 4. K. R. R., one Case of DYSENTERY in P.P.C.L.I, and one case of DIARRHOEA in R.E. Among those suffering from DIARRHOEA in R.E.	First appearance of Gastro-Intestinal disturbance. ENTERIC case was removed straight from billet to Clearing Hospital at BAILLEUL.

(73989) W4141-463. 400,000. 9/14. H.&S.Ltd. Forms/C. 2118/10.

WAR DIARY
or
INTELLIGENCE SUMMARY.
(Erase heading not required.)

Army Form C. 2118.

Hour, Date, Place	Summary of Events and Information	Remarks and references to Appendices
Jan. 11.1915. (cont)	from Ypres, were LIEUT. R. IRELAND & 3 KRR, and CAPT. M.L.S. CLEMENTS, and LIEUTS. S. FEARAND, and C. DAVIES of 4 KRR. The Battalion which chiefly suffered was the 4 K.R.R.	wounded 9.
Jan: 12. -	132 Cases admitted on this day, of which 9 were wounded while all Battalions were represented the 4 K.R.R. had by far the majority. One case each of DIARRHOEA and DYSENTERY are included, also one case of PNEUMONIA.	wounded 18.
Jan. 13. -	93 Cases admitted, including 18 wounded. LIEUT. J.P.MOON, 1 WESSEX: R:E. SORETHROAT is included. Also included is one case of mumps, and afterwards confirmed, ENTERIC FEVER from R.F.A. 1 Case of DYSENTERY – 1R.SCOTS, 1 – 83rd F. AMBULANCE. Drawn I. LEINSTER, one in R.E. and one in 2. CAMERON. H'DERS. The majority of cases admitted, of which 10 were wounded. The number of Ypres cases shews a decided diminution.	wounded 10.
Jan. 14. -		

WAR DIARY
or
INTELLIGENCE SUMMARY.
(Erase heading not required.)

Army Form C. 2118.

Hour, Date, Place	Summary of Events and Information	Remarks and references to Appendices
Jan-14-19, 5 (cont)	While there were 16 cases of DYSENTERY and DIARRHOEA, spread fairly amongst the various units. LIEUT. HER. BERT. CAMPBELL of 4 KRR & is returned – DIARRHOEA.	GASTRO-INTESTINAL cases reach 16.
15. —	Cases admitted 110, of which 27 were wounded, 63 "ghonie" and 4 GASTRO-INTESTINAL	Wounded. 27. G.I. = 4
16. —	96 Cases were admitted to day, of which 21 were wounded and 10 GASTRO-INTESTINAL. The majority of the wounded remainder being "EXPOSURE". LIEUT. H.D. CURTIS, 4 K.R.R. was wounded in face. LIEUT. F. MINCHIN of PPCLI, ulcerated throat.	Wounded. 21. GI = 10.
17. "	105. Cases were admitted this day, of which 18 were wounded including 2ⁿᵈ LIEUT. SPINK. 2 K.S.L.I. 66 "ghonies", including 2ⁿᵈ LIEUTˢ R. APPLEBY, 1ˢᵗ R. Scots and PAT. FITZGERALD, 3 KRR and 8 DYSENTERY. 2ⁿᵈ LIEUT. NORMAN YOUNG. 1 R. Scots and 2ⁿᵈ LIEUT. G. WALMSLEY. (? ENTERIC.) 3. K.R.R.	Wounded. 310 GI. = 8
Jan. 18 — — — —	158 Cases were admitted on this day, of whom 18 were wounded, including LIEUT. AMD RITCHIE. 1 A + SH. 43 "ghonies" and 12 GASTRO-INTESTINAL Cases. LIEUT. S. L. WEBBER, DCLI was admitted with MALARIA.	Wounded. 18. GT 12

Army Form C. 2118.

WAR DIARY
or
INTELLIGENCE SUMMARY.
(Erase heading not required.)

Hour, Date, Place	Summary of Events and Information	Remarks and references to Appendices
Jan. 19. 1915.	74 Cases were admitted today, of which 13 were wounded. 37 were "Spoonu", and 3 Cases GASTRO: INTESTINAL. CAPT. H.W. HEEKAN. 1 LEINSTER. was wounded.	Wounded 13. G-I. 3
Jan. 20. 1915.	198 Cases were admitted of which 14 were wounded. "Spoonu", and 23 GASTRO: INTESTINAL. 132 were	wounded. 14 G.I. 23
Jan. 21. 1915.	113 Cases were admitted, of which 4 were wounded. were "Spoonus" and 9 GASTRO-INTESTINAL. CAPT. G. MOCKETT. and LIEUT. EPIGOTT. 9 R.I., and LIEUT. E. MACDONALD. and LIEUT. G. BIDIE 13 were wounded.	wounded 4 G.I. 9
Jan. 22. 1915.	163 Cases were admitted, of which 13 were wounded. 100 were "Spoonu", and 29 GASTRO-INTESTINAL. CAPT. LOWRY. J.M. 2ᴺᴰ DCLI. Spoonu. sickness.	wounded 13 G.I. 29
Jan. 23. 1915.	79 Cases admitted of which 6 were wounded, 26 were in 4 Spoonu, and 29 GASTRO-INTESTINAL.	wounded 6 G.I. 29
Jan. 24. 1915.	28 Cases admitted, of which 7 were wounded, 4 were Spoonu, and 10 GASTRO-INTESTINAL.	wounded 7 GI 10

7.

WAR DIARY
or
INTELLIGENCE SUMMARY.
(Erase heading not required.)

Army Form C. 2118.

Hour, Date, Place	Summary of Events and Information	Remarks and references to Appendices
Jan. 25. 19/15.	65 Cases were admitted of which 12 were reported in enemy officers, including LIEUT. S.L. JONES, 2y aw officers, including LIEUT D. GRAY, PPCLI and 14 GASTRO-INTESTINAL.	however adm. 12. 1/14. G.I.
Jan. 26. 1915	121 Cases admitted, of which however 7, including LIEUT. J.V. LEES. Epsom 72. GASTRO. INTESTINAL 21 including LIEUT. L. SIDEBOTTOM, 2 DCLI "Epsom 7."	however 7. G.I. 21.
Jan. 27. 1915 to noon	17 Cases admitted of which 5 were wounded, including MAJ. H.C.C. MACNEN GASTRO-INTESTINAL 2. including 83. F² AMB. On 16 & 27 of Jan? at noon, I handed over the station to the 81st 2nd Ambulance. diseases "Exposure" include Frostbite. Swollen feet, Rheumatism. GASTRO-INTESTINAL diseases include ENTERIC FEVER, DYSENTERY, and DIARRHOEA. While it appears that a few hours in the trenches was sufficient to make any personal observation of swollen feet began after	however 5. G.I. 2. ENTERIC FEVER

WAR DIARY or INTELLIGENCE SUMMARY

Army Form C. 2118.

(Erase heading not required.)

Hour, Date, Place	Summary of Events and Information	Remarks and references to Appendices

The night of Jan. 8–9th, or after 48 hours in the trenches. The present Supporting Battalion was the 4th K.R.R. who I believe spent 72 hours on end in the water in the trenches, leaving a direct ratio to 16 hours spent. The cases having many cases at this date were all to say although on an 4th that they generally appeared at the start Dressing Station for evacuation to ~~BAILLEUL~~ CLEAR ING HOSPITAL after their not visit to the Trenches. The inside of JANUARY shows the greatest incidence of cases.

GASTRO-INTESTINAL cases first appeared on the 5th day after trenches were occupied, Jan. 11, when the first case of ENTERIC was notified. This case was probably infected before DICKEBUSCH was occupied; and there have been sporadic cases ever since. The condition of the bowel water traced [points?] to the cause of this disease, although

WAR DIARY
or
INTELLIGENCE SUMMARY.
(Erase heading not required.)

Army Form C. 2118.

Hour, Date, Place	Summary of Events and Information	Remarks and references to Appendices

The men were paraded & warned against drinking water unboiled. I believe the anti-typhoid inoculation has saved the Division from a severe epidemic. All wounded men were inoculated with the anti-tetanic serum as soon as possible, and no case of tetanus has occurred so far.

The recruits taken informed the feet swelling, and the recruits which follow seem to be having fault. For the cases are demanding. Another seems no doubt is the presence of the fittest I have most reliable, having been sent to Clearing Hospital. Therefore the question of acid legis works to feet, and wrapping in blankets. Iodation & iodine injection, I cannot suggest the feet be sweated..... ruins to encourage the return of the blood from the feet.

G. A. S. Rees L.C.
Oc 83rd Fd Ambulance.
Feb. 2/15

Running note.

Confidential

War Diary
 from
Admission and
Discharge Book of
83rd Field Ambulance

G Aldsell Lt. Col
 Of 83rd Field Amb

Feb 2/15
Reninghels

Aus.

Confidential

121/5320

War Diary

of

83rd Field Ambulance, R.A.M.C.

From 21st April, 1915.
To 30th April, 1915.

Vol IV

Diary for 83 & 7A Divisions for Feb + March from 1st to 20th April 1915 inclusive has been applied for

April 13.

There is no change to then Yes to the Period 16 – 20.
Batterys – When the 7a was at L'Allie for – L's Byg – c
to be & will def me 70 + was suceded 3 ? — all week
quiet.

Army Form C. 2118.

WAR DIARY
-or-
INTELLIGENCE SUMMARY
(Erase heading not required.)

Instructions regarding War Diaries and Intelligence Summaries are contained in F.S. Regs, Part II. and the Staff Manual respectively. Title pages will be prepared in manuscript.

Hour, Date, Place	Summary of Events and Information	Remarks and references to Appendices
L'ABBÉ FARM CROMBEKE ROAD nr POPERINGHE		
April 21 – 8 a.m.	Lt Col: G.A. SOULS M.D. O.C. 83rd 3 Amb: left for England leave on medical grounds.	
12 noon	Number for last 24 hours admitted – Officers 15 – Sick 38. Sick: B. Duty 8. Remained 108 of which G.	
22 p.m.	Admitted 8 wounded – 60 sick. Sick B. Duty 59. Remained 116. A report brought by a corporal to M.O. of another unit of a retreat of the allies to some divide, on approach of gas attack. Sick duty. Sent Lieut: DEVONALD POPERINGHE to enquire. He Bn.T return with a that the F.A.D Ambulance should pack + be ready to move. This was done. Some officers + men of 81st Field Ambulance arrived at the billets, and we gave them shelter for the night.	
23 a.8.	Night passed uneventfully. Major IRVINE, called, and officer RAMC then of 81st 3. Amb: left. The unit carried out usual its normal work.	

Army Form C. 2118.

WAR DIARY
or
INTELLIGENCE SUMMARY
(Erase heading not required.)

Instructions regarding War Diaries and Intelligence Summaries are contained in F. S. Regs., Part II. and the Staff Manual respectively. Title pages will be prepared in manuscript.

Hour, Date, Place	Summary of Events and Information	Remarks and references to Appendices
L'HOBE FARM nr POPERINGHE		
April 23 - 12 noon	Admitted 22 sick. Discharged to Cas: Clg. Sta.: 35, to duty 1 - Remained 102 -	
— 24 6 a.m.	The enemy brought gas(?) as(?) of situation -	
	About 8.5in shells fell - No military assets(?) effects.	
	POPERINGHE bombarded -	
9 a.m.	Received orders from ADMS to be ready to take to cottages.9 Arrangements made accordingly -	
12 noon	Admitted 1 officer & 21 NCOs wounded & 36 sick - Disch. to Cas: Clg.Sta. 4 - 11 wounded 9 man died - Remained 155 -	
8 p.m.	Capt STURROCK R.A.M.C. Liaison Army collected wounded with 40 bearers -	
— 25 10 a.m.	Major IRVINE admitted. Evacuation of all patients unable to march.	
12 noon	Admitted 46 wounded and 1 officer & 22 sick - Disch. to Cas. Clg. Sta.: 3 officers and 186 men. Remained 1 officer & 80 men.	
1 p.m.	POPERINGHE again shelled. The gun appears to be of large calibre. No known casualties except among Civilians. No damage to military stores &c.	

1247 W 3299 200,000 (E) 8/14 J.B.C. & A. Form C. 2118/11.

WAR DIARY
or
INTELLIGENCE SUMMARY
(Erase heading not required.)

Army Form C. 2118.

Hour, Date, Place	Summary of Events and Information	Remarks and references to Appendices
L'ABBE FARM n POPERINGHE		
April 26. 10 a.m.	Received orders for ADMS to resume work for 2nd Div.t. Dep.t.	
12.30 p.m.	Transferred Bus. 6 wounded + 83 sick - Sick: 5 Cos: Off.Sgt.: 100 m.sd. 1 man died. Remained 1 officer and 162 m.s.n.	
4.30 p.m.	Heavy shelling of POPERINGHE.	
6 p.m.	ADMS 27th Div.; site DADMS and staff made his Headquarters at this billet.	
—27. 12 noon	Transferred 16 wounded + 1 officer + 20 sick - 5 oth. Cas.: Clg. Sta.: 46, 8 duty 33 - Remained 2 officers + 119 m.s.n.	
6 p.m.	Bombardment of POPERINGHE - and again at 10 p.m.	
8 p.m.	Lieuts J.S.R. BOYD and RENNY collected with 40 bearers. The carry was in each case considerable.	
10.30 p.m.	Lieut A. DEVONALD went out with six cars to the direction of YPRES to help in loading.	

WAR DIARY
or
INTELLIGENCE SUMMARY

(Erase heading not required.)

Army Form C. 2118.

Hour, Date, Place	Summary of Events and Information	Remarks and references to Appendices

L'ABBE FARM
nr POPERINGHE

April 28. 3 a.m. — Lieut. KENNY having rejoined his unit, Lieut: C.A. BOYD rejoined this unit.

11. a.m. — Lieut. M.C. HAYWARD M.B. from 2/3 Home Counties F. Amb. rejoined this unit.

12 noon — Had transferred us 2 wounded & 5 sick. Disch: & Cas: Clg: St: 1 Officer 44 N.C.O. Remained 1 Officer 9122 N.C.O.

29. 12 noon — No patients were admitted or transferred. 4 wounded & 11 sick were discharged to Cas: Clg: St. & 15 N.C.O. to D.of.S. Remained 1 Officer 9097 N.C.O.

30. 11 a.m. — Received orders to proceed to offer back as a strong station. Arrangements made accordingly.

12 noon — Transferred to us 8 sick. Died: & 9 & 11. Remained 1 Officer + 94 N.C.O.

8 p.m. — LIEUTS: DEVONALD, C.A. BOYD, & HAYWARD collected & HE 36 beard. Rather heavy night.

121/5556

24th Division

83rd Field Ambulance

Vol V

121/5556

May 1915

WAR DIARY
or
INTELLIGENCE SUMMARY

(Erase heading not required.)

Army Form C. 2118.

Hour, Date, Place	Summary of Events and Information	Remarks and references to Appendices
L'ABBÉ FARM nr POPERINGHE May 1		
12 noon	Still acts as a dressing station.	
	Admitted 1 officer & 47 msn wounded & 7 officer & 25 msn sick. Sent to Cas: Coll: Sta: 2 officer & 53 msn - & duty 13 msn - 1 mar died of wounds - Remained 1 officer & 100 msn -	
2 11—	Assumed work as a Conv: Depot - Nw 82nd F Amb: Ford	
	a Dressing Stn in POPERINGHE -	
12 noon	Admitted 5 officers & 46 wounded and 4 officer & 6 sick - Sick. to Cas: Coll: Sta: 6 officer & 1 msn, to duty 2 msn - 2 msn died of wounds. Remained 1 officer & 127 msn.	
11 p.m.	Visit: DEVONALD sent to POTYSE with Car - 6 Car -	
3 3 a.m.	Visit: CA. BOYD sent up to YPRES with Car -	
12 noon	Admitted 21 msn wounded & 7 officer & 58 msn sick - Sent to Cas: Coll: Sta: 4 msn - & duty 1 officer & 18 msn - 1 officer & msn - Remained 1 officer & 184 msn -	

Army Form C. 2118.

WAR DIARY
or
INTELLIGENCE SUMMARY
(Erase heading not required.)

Instructions regarding War Diaries and Intelligence Summaries are contained in F. S. Regs., Part II. and the Staff Manual respectively. Title pages will be prepared in manuscript.

Hour, Date, Place	Summary of Events and Information	Remarks and references to Appendices
L'ABEE FARM nr POPERINGHE		
May 3 (cont). 7.30p.m.	Lieuts C.A. BOYD & J.S.R. BOYD started with 40 bearers – also one the night of the 2nd started to N.S.W. trenches, and it was anxious work for the bearers well carried out –	
4. 12 noon	Transferred to 4 wounded + 72 sick – of whom 29 were suffering from the effects of poisonous gas – Sent to Cas. Clg. Stn: 61 men. Remained 1 Officer + 168 men. POPERINGHE again shelled with different shells –	
5. 3. a.m. 10 a.m. 12 noon	Lieut HAYWARD starting with 20 bearers. Sustained 3 casualties. POPERINGHE shelled. Transferred to 2 Officers + 32 men wounded + 1 Officer + 47 men sick – of whom two are suffering from effects of poisonous gas. – Sent to Cas. Clg. Stn: 1 Officer + 16 men – & 105 48 m.r. (Armed) 2 Officers + 484 men.	
2 p.m.	Lieuts DESMOND + J.S.R. BOYD sent out to collect with 40 bearers. The new carrying and arduous work are considerable physical strain –	

WAR DIARY or INTELLIGENCE SUMMARY

Army Form C. 2118.

Hour, Date, Place	Summary of Events and Information	Remarks and references to Appendices
L'ABBÉ FARM nr POPERINGHE		
May 6 — 12 noon	Admitted to dress transferred & wounded and 1 Officer & 62 men sick — of whom 30 were suffering from effects of poisonous gas. Sent to Cas: Clg: Stn: 1 Officer & 38 men — 8 O.R. 38 men. One man died from asphyxiation. Remained 2 Officers & 73 men.	
7.30 p.m.	Night: HAYWARD collected with 25 bearers wounded 2 casualties.	
	During the night the 82nd Field Ambulance were shelled out of their dressing station in POPERINGHE & evacuated all their cases. We took in a few wounded.	
?) 12 noon	Admitted to dress transferred 26 wounded & 1 Officer & 107 sick — of whom 9 were cases of gas poisoning. Sent to Cas: Clg: Stn: 5 — 8 O.R.s. One man died from asphyxiation. Remained 3 Officers & 29 men.	
7 p.m.	Visits: C. A. BOYD & J.S.R. BOYD collected with 3 N.C.O.s & 36 bearers. Better arrangements for collecting wounded were being made esp: by B⁰ the Brigade. Cars taken to BIRR X R⁰⁰	

1247 W 3299 200,000 (E) 8/14 J.B.C. & A. Forms/C. 2118/11. T.O. 085 –

Army Form C. 2118.

WAR DIARY
or
INTELLIGENCE SUMMARY
(Erase heading not required.)

Instructions regarding War Diaries and Intelligence Summaries are contained in F. S. Regs., Part II. and the Staff Manual respectively. Title pages will be prepared in manuscript.

Hour, Date, Place	Summary of Events and Information	Remarks and references to Appendices
LABBE FARM nr POPERINGHE		
May 7 (cont) 9.30pm	31 shells thrown into POPERINGHE and surrounding and some did not explode.	
8.	Weather which had been warm summerlike continued hot. About 10 a.m. shell cannonading obsy the transit front of our front Ward continued all by slight intervals till 6 p.m. During this time a Bssolty bombardment of POPERINGHE vicinity carried on. The largest life of guns afforward to be used again.	
12 noon	Trans find Btes. 4 wounded and 1 Officer + 67 men Sick. Sent 945: 2 Officers + 40 men — Bgs: Cy. St: 2 Officer + 29 men — Bgs: 2 Officer + 40 men — Astrained 246 men.	

WAR DIARY or INTELLIGENCE SUMMARY

Army Form C. 2118.

Hour, Date, Place	Summary of Events and Information	Remarks and references to Appendices
L'ABBÉ FARM nr POPERINGHE		
May 8	During the day reports of heavy fighting with severe losses on both sides began to arrive. Received orders to be off hand to take in wounded. Arrangements made accordingly. Only 1 convoy of 9 wounded arrived, having (apart from the slight cases recently taken in) and the night passed uneventfully.	
9 a.m.	Lieut DEVONALD sent to BRANDHOEK with 1 N.C.O. & 20 bearers. There was a heavy night's work.	
May 9 –		
12 noon	Admitted & had transfers 1 officer & 7 n.c.o. (wounded) — 45 sick – Disch: to Conc: Cp: Stn: & 32 – Evac'd 1 officer Remained 278. Orders received from ADMS — (1) To keep numbers as low as possible to 200 limit. (2) To report cases of infective riv. or injuries treatment. These are in future to be sent for expert advice to ARQUES.	
12.30 p.m.	Service with one or other Dev'n Ambulance of the Division whose Staffs for were temporarily billeted with this unit. These officers were subsequently attached to the unit by A.D.M.S. Visitors: R.G.J. McEntire M.B., W.W. Scholess	

WAR DIARY
or
INTELLIGENCE SUMMARY

Army Form C. 2118.

Hour, Date, Place	Summary of Events and Information	Remarks and references to Appendices
L'ABBÉ FARM nr POPERINGHE May 9	POPERINGHE & neighbourhood were shelled during the day. No cases of gas poisoning had come in for 2 days. Of those which passed through our hands the most had a rapid suffocating anoxia resorting. In some the effect was more serious, and, after the patient by any showed the symptoms of an acute bronchitis. The men who died, died from asphyxiation. It was impossible to deduce the exact % which died from disintegration of lung tissue etc. Deaths were throughout these facilities. Mortality was a little under 5 per cent. — This unit was charged with the work of making masks. Material supplies from GHQ. Patients were employed in the work which was supervised by Lieut. J.S.K. BOYD. Up to date 4,600 masks have been made to be sufficiently to hyposulphide of sodium solution by the troops. Also this day Lieut. BOYD began the preparation of ? filter tow? etc. of a solution of Na₂CO₃ + hyposulphide which is to be used for spraying the trenches. —	
7.30 /A.	Visits: HAYWARD and VENABLES were out with 2 NCOs + 24 trans. Supplement 82nd A.A.G. It was a fairly heavy nights work, with a large proportion of static out. 1000 additional masks were sent of hyposulphide at the same time.	

Army Form C. 2118.

WAR DIARY
or
INTELLIGENCE SUMMARY
(Erase heading not required.)

Instructions regarding War Diaries and Intelligence Summaries are contained in F. S. Regs., Part II. and the Staff Manual respectively. Title pages will be prepared in manuscript.

Hour, Date, Place	Summary of Events and Information	Remarks and references to Appendices
ABEELE FARM nr POPERINGHE May 10 (cont) 12 (noon)	Had transferred 3 wounded + 13 sick - Sick: to C.o.; Offr: 51. O. Rs: 61 - O. Rs: 7. 45. Remained 188. No carts of our patients were rec'd - Lt C.A. BOYD proceeded to BRANDHOEK Station in passing -	
8 p.m.	Sent up to the troops 32 Sprays with gauze & cotton wool for use — Lamber of Officers & NCOs & men of other Units (of England) visited us to day — Nothing for writing of POPERINGHE during the day.	
11.12.45 am	Received orders from ADMS (Ban-Indies) through DDMS from G.O.C. VII Army (copy) to proceed with the work of road making in neighbourhood of Lt J.S.K. BOYD got together 12 orderlies who carried through the work to the R.A.M.C. other patients were drawn in by the work. Material was also given out by women of the neighbourhood.	
9.10 a.m.	A rifle bombardment of POPERINGHE began. Officers & for a part of our practice small calibre. The shells (German) fell in the gardens of the town. A few did not explode. (Lasted 20 minutes.	
12 noon.	Admitted or had transferred to 6 wounded and 3 Sick: 5 R.C.H- 5. duty 51 - Remained 219. Class St: 23.	
4 p.m.	Sent up to Adm. HQrs 2) Lt. Bowser 2100 Respirators and 17 Sprays with Sharpe Solution - nr CENTRE HQrs - Assist. DEVONALD, MAYNARD, and _____ collected with 70 experts and 3 R.C.O.S.	

WAR DIARY
or
INTELLIGENCE SUMMARY

(Erase heading not required.)

Army Form C. 2118.

Instructions regarding War Diaries and Intelligence Summaries are contained in F. S. Regs., Part II. and the Staff Manual respectively. Title pages will be prepared in manuscript.

Hour, Date, Place	Summary of Events and Information	Remarks and references to Appendices
ABEELE FARM nr POPERINGHE May 11 (cont). 10.30 p.m.	Lt. REISS of 81st 3 Amb. returned to our bivy that Lieut HAYWARD had been wounded by shrapnel, appearing in tone of R. bag. General condition said to be satisfactory. Lieuts of ADMS to send an officer to the place. Sgr Lieut: VENABLES.	
12 6 a.m.	POPERINGHE again shelled with 7 shells of (different) calibres distributed. The Bearer pot has Lt. DENOTAD, Sgr to Bearer, left at the East & Bivy: & Lt. HAYWARD wounded, returns reports that one bearer had also been wounded.	
12 (noon)	Admin: transf: Wounded 2 officers + 24 m.n., sick 1. Sent to Cas. C.St., 1 officer + 37 m.n. 8 sgt-S. 1 officer + 9 m.n. remained.	
2.30 p.m. 3...	205. A.F.a shells thrown into POPERINGHE. Some did not explode. 2,500 more respirators sent to Bn: Hqs for distribution to the Coops. Of these 900·0 were made at HAZEBROOK, 800 by the 82nd Fd. Amb. and 200 here. Also 16 cases of Coln. to forward those were sent.	

Army Form C. 2118.

WAR DIARY
or
INTELLIGENCE SUMMARY
(Erase heading not required.)

Instructions regarding War Diaries and Intelligence Summaries are contained in F. S. Regs., Part II. and the Staff Manual respectively. Title pages will be prepared in manuscript.

Hour, Date, Place		Summary of Events and Information	Remarks and references to Appendices
VIEUX FARM AT POPERINGHE			
May 12 (am)	11 p.m.	Lieut. DEFONARD and 1 Sgt. r6 theirs returned from the École where they had been on duty today. Total turn of 16f 30 hour. Reports that numerous casualties are still coming in.	
		Home red came in during the night.	
		After arranged bombing from HAZEBROOK 2000 more troops forward to 27th and 28th Divisions.	
13	12 noon	Had transferred that 17 wounded, 46 sick. Sent to Cas. Cl. Sta. 26, & duty	
		28. Remained 21)	
	8 p.m.	Capt. STURROCK went up to BRANDHOEK Staff with Dressings	
	10 p.m.	9 Skills done staff etc. at POPERINGHE & Wright Mouchard. Some destruction	
14		Who is set for night it our still cold rainy.	
	12 noon	Admitted to new Conv. Camp 1 Officer & 16 wounded. 1 Officer & 31 Sick.	
		Sent to Cas. Cl. Sta. 1 Officer returns. May 23. Admitted 1 Officer & 31	
	6.30 p.m.	Lieut. C.J.A. BOYD, J.S.M. BOYD, & McENTIRE collects with 4 N.C.O. & 166 horses.	
		From a somewhat lighted night work. There were no casualties among the	
	8 p.m.	brass.	
		Lt. Gr.M. ricard Tracy that Lieut. BROCK RAMC attacked R.I. succeeds.	
		had been wounded. Lieut. VENABLES detailed to take his place.	

Army Form C. 2118.

WAR DIARY
or
INTELLIGENCE SUMMARY

(Erase heading not required.)

Instructions regarding War Diaries and Intelligence Summaries are contained in F. S. Regs., Part II. and the Staff Manual respectively. Title pages will be prepared in manuscript.

Hour, Date, Place	Summary of Events and Information	Remarks and references to Appendices
L'EBBÉ FARM — nr POPERINGHE		
May 15		
5 a.m.	Lieut: JSR. BOYD and McENTIRE returned with 3 NCOs & 60 Bomrs. Lieut: C.A. BOYD and 1 NCO to obtain train, having been left with the ECOLE. (Lieut: BOYD reports that while satisfactory arrangements are being made on the left side, on account of the difficulty of officers collecting & informing the relay race & other arrangements & are short of who do not know the ralay race & other arrangements complete. He recommends that, as (i) Regts ad joint are containing charge of (ii) they are about to take over (iii) one or two known collecting posts seem to be difficult to provide. One or two known collecting posts to be established on the right as on the left. Brothers Reggie Fitches Bearers should carry carro awaiting evacuation immediately after dark.	
12 noon.	Hon. of our cas: 2 offrs ws wounded & 3 offrs & 77 sects. S.m.r gas. cl st. 1 offrs. r42. R.gs 1 — Removed 4 offrs r262.	
4 p.m.	Lieut: J.C. TYPER M.B., S.R. joined the unit in place of Lieut: HAYWARD wounded.	
10 p.m.	Lieut: C.A. BOYD returned with 1 NCO & 6 Bomrs, having carried through 28 h.w. Ten of July, reports a fairly light Boys' work. POPERINGHE was now shelled for 3 to day & night. Gilbert commander became heavy about 9 p.m. Removed to the blvr of days by night. Gal. rather unsettled weather continued.	

1247 W 3299 200,000 (E) 8/14 J.B.C. & A. Forms/C. 2118/11.

WAR DIARY
INTELLIGENCE SUMMARY
(Erase heading not required.)

Army Form C. 2118.

Hour, Date, Place	Summary of Events and Information	Remarks and references to Appendices

L'ABBE FARM
Nr POPERINGHE

May 16. 12 noon
Adm. or Transf: 2 wounded, 150 Sick. So rts Cas, old est. 52. 3 Officers 443, 2 July 16. Remained 1 Officer & 255.
A good deal of aerial reconnaissance took place in the afternoon. Later some heavy cannonading began. Lists though the night.
About 30 slight cases were admitted during the night.

17 - 12 noon
Adm. or Transf: 11 wounded. 48 Sick. 48 July Co. Remained 1 officer & 173 men. Lieuts: DEVONALD, McENTIRE, HYDER returned with 3 Russel and 48 Reservists.
Rain and heavy casualty throughout the night. On the 2nd Lt DEVONALD reported that it has been a light night's work. When the men left the farm to report shelling. One bearer had, however, been caught by a shrapnel bullet. Casualty had been forwarded and did not arrive here above the day. Lt. PEMBERS with 1 NCO & 8 men left at the ECOLE.

18. 8am
31 slight cases were received here during the night. A few shots were fired at POPERINGHE. No reports of fell homicide on the far side of the town.

Army Form C. 2118.

WAR DIARY
or
INTELLIGENCE SUMMARY

(Erase heading not required.)

Instructions regarding War Diaries and Intelligence Summaries are contained in F. S. Regs., Part II. and the Staff Manual respectively. Title pages will be prepared in manuscript.

Hour, Date, Place	Summary of Events and Information	Remarks and references to Appendices
LIEBEE FARM NEAR POPERINGHE May 18.	The following memo received from O.C. No 61 Fld Amb.	
12 noon	Conduct of Pte: MARTIN and MIFFLIN of your Ambulance whilst under my orders in POTIGE from 21st April 8 to 7th May, firing that time they performed work of the most "" a nature of great value and always showed the greatest "gay"	
10.30 p.m.	3 wounded + 33 Sick. Died 8 Sgt 8. Remained 201	
	Rem a war transf. 3 wounded.	
	Lt. McENTIRE returned with NCO & six hours reports of quiet day. During the day & night wounded & sick taken. Transferred 1 wounded, & officer + Sgt sick. Sent to O.C. Cdy. Stn. 11 officer and 62 — 8 officers duty 40 - Remained 145 -	
19. 12 noon	Lt. GRIFFITHS who had opened the forward dressing room, reporting billeted with the unit today. Caught of the A.D.M.S. sent to 8.2.03 & No 1 Ambulance.	
20. 12 noon	Transferred 6 sick - 4 wounded. one officer - 30 sick - Sent to No 22. Remained 1 officer + 158. POPERINGHE was twice bombarded during the day. May shells did notable some FW ade of the town.	

WAR DIARY
or
INTELLIGENCE SUMMARY

(Erase heading not required.)

Army Form C. 2118.

Hour, Date, Place	Summary of Events and Information	Remarks and references to Appendices
IGGLE FARM nr POPERINGHE May 20	The following were admitted [to?] Antoinette martin in hospital S/Sgt: SPIELMAN Re: by Lieut C.A.BOYD Pte: SEARLE Pte: MUMFORD (cyclist) ... and Lt. McDONALD S/Sgt: INGE ... Lt. McDONALD Pte: MARTIN ... Lt: G.W. GREENE (Flot 2 Amb) Pte: MIFFLIN	
7.30 p.m.	Lieut C.A.BOYD, J/Sgt BOYD, +YPER attacked with 3 NCOs and 40 bearers. It was a light night work. Lt J.C.R. BOYD remained with 6 men at the Ecole. Only the right side of hospital is now a [illegible]. More than usual no. of lying sitting cases carried. Able amount of rifle fire - two rounds were answered by rifle bullets.	
May 21 12 noon	Lt. McENTIRE sent to St Omer for some of the spares to Corp 3000 respirators to Div. Hqs. Transferred forms 8 Extra X.D. and 42 sick - Sgt Clark Ug 82 27 - beds 24 - remained 146 -	

WAR DIARY
or
INTELLIGENCE SUMMARY

(Erase heading not required.)

Army Form C. 2118.

Instructions regarding War Diaries and Intelligence Summaries are contained in F. S. Regs, Part II. and the Staff Manual respectively. Title pages will be prepared in manuscript.

Hour, Date, Place	Summary of Events and Information	Remarks and references to Appendices
May 21 (cont'd) 10.30 a.m. POPERINGHE	Lt. J.S.A. BOYD returned with horses having been on duty with Scots Guards today. Tel train of Feb 28 horse H guns boys. The escort for draft of drafts in return POPERINGHE - of which 6 arrived to be fitted.	
22 11 a.m.	Visit of Brigadier J. KEOGH from 3 Home Counties F.A.Bde., formed the Unit on Parade.	
12 noon	Adm. order transferred 10 o.r.s. and 1 officer +65 seat. Camp to Co. Cy. St. 34, to Duty 31. Remained 1 officer +36.	
10 p.m.	After a cannonade of guns hard during the afternoon, rather sever on our Rear, lasting about 2 hours. A terrific thunder & lightning storm broke out at Evening. Vivid flashes of lightning.	
23 10 a.m.	A few shells were thrown into POPERINGHE. Wrote to A.D.M.S. for 5 or that Sergt. SMITHSON + Corp. CARR were sufficiently fit to our establishment wishing to return to the other them.	
12 noon	Lt. DEPORKO called my attention to Circular Memorandum of Director of Transport No. 11 of 25/2/15 advising for permits of Horse Transport Personnel on Probation. Advised Lt. DEPORKO to before a list of suitable promotions.	* D of T No. 1842

1247 W 3299 200,000 (E) 8/14 J.B.C. & A. Forms/C. 2118/11.

WAR DIARY or INTELLIGENCE SUMMARY

Form C. 2118.

Hour, Date, Place	Summary of Events and Information	Remarks and references to Appendices
L'EBBE FARM n-POPERINGHE May 23 - (Sun)	Divine Service was held at 11.30 a.m. conducted by Pr: W. GRIFFIN. Was followed by a celebration of Holy Communion.	
12 noon	Adm. of transf(?) arranged. 14 officer + 58 other ranks Sent. 8 Refs 3 - 1 Officer + 196 mv. remaining.	
8 p.m.	Lieut. McENTIRE + 2 NCOs proceeded to the scale to be in a position to give information to those who were taking over the work, of that sect. He returned at 2 a.m. reported that the guides provided seemed well acting with tolerable efficiency + that there had been no very clear indication of the need for his services.	
May 24.	Arty. and commanding began at 1 a.m. in which it was difficult to distinguish between the gases of the allies replying through the night. On entered - almost without intermission through the night became typical rates about 9 a.m.	
1.30 a.m.	Phone from BARTH S that the enemy troops had been reported East of YPRES. All units should be ordered (or stand by) for instructions. The a-ly(?), be ready to man order to mount (below, the a-standard (but no horses used) be a-standard".	

1247 W 3299 200,000 (E) 8/14 J.B.C. & A. Forms/C. 2118/11.

Army Form C. 2113.

WAR DIARY
or
INTELLIGENCE SUMMARY

(Erase heading not required.)

Instructions regarding War Diaries and Intelligence Summaries are contained in F. S. Regs., Part II. and the Staff Manual respectively. Title pages will be prepared in manuscript.

Hour, Date, Place	Summary of Events and Information	Remarks and references to Appendices
I'ZOOE FARM nr POPERINGHE May 24 (AM D) 7.30 a.m.	Instructions for scavenging:— (1) M.O's (Major BARTLEY and Lieut. C.A. BOYD) to report as soon as possible the number of patients unable to march 10 miles. (2) NCOs in charge of (a) Bearers (b) Drivers and (c) Company to provide some ballast material absolutely necessary for camp on moving out. The remainder to be packed in the wagons. (3) Men to pack their kits. (4) Patients not to draw their kits till the latest. (5) Cooking utensils to be left out till the latest. Arrange till the same time that DM&MC tent should not be struck till he had returned.	
8.30 a.m.	By order of DADMS Lieut PIPER to report at HQs for Service with 2nd Bn. R.S.C.I until their own M.O returned from leave.	
12 noon	Adm on Tamst 1 wounded up(sick) Sent to the Cy St. 2 officers + 34 n.s.r. to day 13.— Remained 167.	

WAR DIARY or INTELLIGENCE SUMMARY

Army Form C. 2118.

Hour, Date, Place	Summary of Events and Information	Remarks and references to Appendices
LIEBRE FARM nr POPERINGHE		
May 24, 1915 (cont) 8 p.m.	Received orders from S.A.D.M.S. to send 1 officer & 24 bearers to the ECOLE to be in charge & in care of Shropleys; & 1 officer & 18 bearers to BRANDHOEK for such of the sick & wounded of Lt. DE ROMAIN & C.A. BOYD who were sent in accordance with these orders, with the necessary number of bearers. During the day Lt. G. HOLMES (81st F. Amb) who had returned to duty from Hospital and had been trained here, returned to the 81st F. Amb.	
May 25 10 p.m.	After the we arrived there in POPERINGHE.	
7:30 a.m.	Received a message from Lt. C. A. BOYD stating that he had been ordered by the G.O.C. 80th Brigade to remain at the LILLE Gate YPRES for the present, that he was mainly there for any orders with the orderlies. Shortly afterwards received a verbal message from Lt. DE ROMAIN that he was also remaining (at the Dress Stn BRANDHOEK?) as the "Do la Brigade" were refused.	
12 noon	to attack. Refres to these messages were sent by S.A.D.M.S. * Refr: 1) for Adm. on F: 29 wounded* & 7 sick - Sent to Cas. Clg Stn: 26. * Rel: 1) for Regt. 15. - Remained 230. Cross —	

Army Form C. 2118.

WAR DIARY
or
INTELLIGENCE SUMMARY
(Erase heading not required.)

Instructions regarding War Diaries and Intelligence Summaries are contained in F.S. Regs, Part II. and the Staff Manual respectively. Title pages will be prepared in manuscript.

Hour, Date, Place	Summary of Events and Information	Remarks and references to Appendices
HEBUE FARM nr POPERINGHE		
May 25. (cont.) 2.30 p.m.	Lt PIPER left to take the place of Lt BEA- MO ABBEELE about that. Lt DESMOND with 1 NCO + 3 bearers returned after an '18 hr' tour of duty. Reported that a considerable number of serious cases had had to be collected. Most of these were shell shock after the fight.	
May 26. 7 a.m.	Informed by DADMS that the 2/Lt Devine would almost immediately be attached to a new formation, and that preparation should be made accordingly - Later in the day it became clear that the move (so far as concerns numbers) was not likely to be immediate. Partial packing of stores fell of often was carried onward. A few tent chocks - With regard to patients wounded etc were sent to 2/3 Fd. Hos. HQrs BUSSEBOOM, a likely large evacuation was hoped for and urgent orders to two HQrs of other Fd. Hos. asking for & holding for 12 hrs 3 each; for instruction and detail.	
12.30 p.m	By order of DADMS 6 waggons to pick up stragglers of 82nd Brigade coming thro' to LOCRE	

WAR DIARY or INTELLIGENCE SUMMARY

Army Form C. 2118.

(Erase heading not required.)

Instructions regarding War Diaries and Intelligence Summaries are contained in F.S. Regs., Part II. and the Staff Manual respectively. Title pages will be prepared in manuscript.

Hour, Date, Place	Summary of Events and Information	Remarks and references to Appendices
LIEBBE FARM nr POPERINGHE May 26 (cont'd)		
12 noon	We also received instruction to continue the manufacture of respirators. All available material was used. About 1000 were turned out under the superintendence of Lt. J.S.R.BOYD, then of Lt. McBRYDE. ADM attd. to 6 Corps S.C.D. 1, 2 Evch - Sent to Car. Cf. Br. 2) - To	
day 33. Remained 206. The day was extremely hot.		
11 a.m.	The BASPMS surrendered 2 horses at Army Cypo to and sent to ADMS 28th Div. Ambulance 2 mules obtained as Sent 1 MO from this unit. Sent Lt. McENTIRE	
12 noon	ADM or transf. 3 sick - Sent to Car. Cf. Sto. 1 officer 402 men.	
	+ Evac 19 - Remained 1 officer 384 men.	
28		
7 a.m.	By order of DADMS at CA-BOYD was sent out with car to pick up note on to LOCRE stragglers from 82nd Brigade.	
12 noon	ADM - Transferred - 22 sick - Sent to Car. Cf. Sto. 1 officer 405 Duty - 38. Remained 12.	
3 p.m.	Lt PYPER rejoined the unit.	

WAR DIARY or INTELLIGENCE SUMMARY

Army Form C. 2118.

(Erase heading not required.)

Hour, Date, Place	Summary of Events and Information	Remarks and references to Appendices
LEBBE FARM nr POPERINGHE May 29. 12 noon	Adm. or T. & 1 gas case and 10 sick. Sent to Cas. Cly. Str. 15. Remained 8 — Various important orders — orders came in for 3 today. That next form 3 *6(B)* to Periscopes (now forming) their (1) should be carried forward than round the road (11) should be of the higher shape, size etc, and that (111) the paper should also be stiffened & the men. Also the plans memo: from the G.O.C. 2) a decision as to advisability of Arms for information from the General commanding the Division asked power to consults to all ranks of the R.A.M.C (T) Units under power on the splendid & devoted work bn many in the Division during the recent heavy fighting. "He has on this act admiration the coolness as has displayed however dangerous whereto the task to be performed. The good results & the manner in which the combatant

WAR DIARY or INTELLIGENCE SUMMARY

(Erase heading not required.)

Army Form C. 2118.

Hour, Date, Place	Summary of Events and Information	Remarks and references to Appendices
1st 86th FAH in POPERINGHE May 29. (cont.)	branches of the Service officers is what has been done for those wounded must be a great satisfaction to you. The Major General heartily congratulates you on all ranks. These Divisional Units have proved that this war in difficult danger to Y. fighters the greater tradition of their comrades in the Regular Service." This rather boring use may return parade the whole field as office officers.	
—30 12.60 a.m.	The day was spent in preparation for departure. Lt J.S.R. BOYD with a lorry proceeded into car (proceeds) to ARMENTIERES to obtain supplies equipment sent in advance. Also in transit 15 sick. 20 cas. Cap. Sir G. Newman to	
—31 7 a.m.	Lt CABOYD with 2 cars proceeded to LOCRE with a small billetting party. The remaining motor cars had orders to follow the Field Ambulance at 1 hour interval.	

WAR DIARY or INTELLIGENCE SUMMARY

Army Form C. 2113.

(Erase heading not required.)

Hour, Date, Place	Summary of Events and Information	Remarks and references to Appendices

LEBBE FARM nr POPERINGHE

May 3. (Sat) 9.a.m. — The 2nd Amblnce with entire transport two motor cars marched via POPERINGHE to ZEVECOTEN. Being 20 minutes before scheduled time, the 2 Amb. had to halt on the near side of RENINGHELST. From ZEVECOTEN to LOCRE the march occupied 50 minutes. (inclusive of 20 minutes halt).

12.15 p.m. — (finish) 9.

LOCRE

12.5 p.m. — Arrived at our bivouac at LOCRE. Reports arrived at Brigade Headquarters sent round Operation Orders for next day. The day might have been more favourably spent in getting the men bivouacked on.

3/m — Lt GODOYD with 2 NCOs were in 2 motor ambulances dragged/proceeded to ARMENTIERES to take over the advanced dressing station from 1 A-Div Amb Corps.

24th Division

187/5991

Confidential

amd

War Diary of

83rd Field Ambulance, R.A.M.C.

from 1st June 1915 to 30th June 1915.

Vol VI

12/5991.

June 1915

Army Form C. 2118.

WAR DIARY
or
INTELLIGENCE SUMMARY
(Erase heading not required.)

Instructions regarding War Diaries and Intelligence Summaries are contained in F.S. Regs, Part II. and the Staff Manual respectively. Title pages will be prepared in manuscript.

Hour, Date, Place	Summary of Events and Information	Remarks and references to Appendices
LOCRE June 1 6 a.m.	Lt PYPER received orders to send one motor waggon via DRANOUTRE without stating 2 waggons ahead of Ambulance As 3 are together. Brigade to tell billets near STEEN MERCKE held up by any stragglers.	
6.20 a.m.	The 3rd Ambulance marched out of LOCRE (to make room), a corresponding half being Meerkens. Thence it proceeded to ARMENTIERES and to reach hut and one long halt of ½ hr on the near side of MEPPE for the purpose of watering and feeding. The 2nd Ambulance reached at Billets at the ECOLE NATIONALE at 11.30.	
8.30 p.m.	Temporary billets were provided for officer rather poor, (the 2nd & 3rd Amb have not yet evacuated the quarters. They did, however, that our sick and our cases as evacuated and collected under Lt PYPER from the Aid Post in the TROUP LINES area.	J.G.Gth

1247   W 3299   200,000   (E)   8/14   J.B.C. & A.   Forms/C. 2118/11.

WAR DIARY
or
INTELLIGENCE SUMMARY
(Erase heading not required.)

Army Form C. 2118.

Hour, Date, Place	Summary of Events and Information	Remarks and references to Appendices
ARMENTIERES June 1 (contd)	The need for POPERINGHE proceeds throughout either an io other. Order is due to the Transport Officer, to DEPONARD for the oversight packing of the buggers & the excellent condition of the horses.	
2. 10 a.m.	Sick were collected for billets.	
	He left at 3 A.M. Hoory left at 2 p.m. The horses surroundings were cleared, and the harness I take for various duties and placed in permanent stalls. Admitted to wounded 14, sick 6, Sent to Case. Cly. Sta. 10, to duty 61, 1 dead. Remained 25.	
12 noon	Much cleaning up & arrange was done in the afternoon.	
8.30/6.	Lt ISABOYD (with Lt SONNTAG & MCARTER who accompanied him for instruction) collected from HOUPLINES with 8 horses. About 30 shells (mainly shrapnel) were dropped in the town in the afternoon. A chile was carried but in the morn. The usual routine was gradually getting into working order.	
3	Last esto blotment is gradually getting into working order.	HGG(?)

WAR DIARY or INTELLIGENCE SUMMARY

Army Form C. 2118.

(Erase heading not required.)

Hour, Date, Place	Summary of Events and Information	Remarks and references to Appendices
ARMENTIERES June 3 (contd.) 12 noon.	Admitted 3 wounded and 2 Officers + 18 sick. Sent to Con: O.S. Remained 2 Officers + 39. Lt. C.A. BOYD reports that the 81st Brigade had extended their line to the ZILLE Railway & were occupying the Aid Post at RATION FARM. He wished to know if there was any object in keeping on the advanced dressing stn at CHAPELLE D'AR- MENTIERES. Acting on instructions from acting A.D.M.S. I went to see the Brig Gen of 80th Brigade who gave me a free hand to prospect for a dressing station in the HOUPLINES area. This was done by Lt. C.A. BOYD on the following day.	
8.30 p.	Lt. ALABASTER collected. There were only a few cases but some were seriously wounded.	
4.12 noon.	Admitted 3 wounded + 20 sick. Sent to Con: Clg Stn. 1 officer and 14. 8 sick. 1 officer + 2. to other Fd Ambs (81st) 8. Remained 40. Rev. A.T. CAPE C.F. (Mis(s)ion) & Rev. P. COMEAU (C.E.) were attached to the unit.	
8.30 p.m.	Lt. SONNTAG collected. Only a few cases were brought in —	HGGH

WAR DIARY or INTELLIGENCE SUMMARY

Army Form C. 2118.

(Erase heading not required.)

Hour, Date, Place	Summary of Events and Information	Remarks and references to Appendices
ARMENTIERES June 5	General Routine was followed. The 50th a troop guards got 2.8 orders.	
8.30 am	The G.O.C. Divn in fact visit to Med: Surgical wards. Lt PYPER collected a few cases.	
12 (noon)	Adm: 4 wounded + 30 sick. Evnt. to Cas: Cl.St. 6 - to Div Rest Stn: 7. to Duty 5. Remained 34.	
June 6 - 12 noon	Adm: 2 wounded; 18 sick. to C.C. Stn - 5. to D.R. Stn 6, to Duty 8. Rsn: 35. The 81st Brigade having taken over the area up to LILLE RLWY, the adv: Dress Stn 3 it was changed out Officers of acting ADMS to a Theatre in Mourz HOOPLINE (C 26 5.9.2) There was no charge of rooms. Received orders to take charge of motors left at a Rest Station at STEENWERCK. Sent Lt DEMONAID of state over. Lt DEMONAID reports that the place was so small for administration 5, 3 & 3 amb. So the NCO who were with him.	
8.30 pm	Lt J.S.R. BOYD collected. There was a postcard, no wounded.	J.G.GM

Army Form C. 2118.

WAR DIARY
or
INTELLIGENCE SUMMARY.
(Erase heading not required.)

Instructions regarding War Diaries and Intelligence Summaries are contained in F. S. Regs., Part II. and the Staff Manual respectively. Title pages will be prepared in manuscript.

Hour, Date, Place	Summary of Events and Information	Remarks and references to Appendices
ARMENTIERES		
June 7 10. a.m.	Under instructions from 6.C. A.D.M.S. (Tanks) to proceed to depôt of Soda Water factories in town. This was done in a most efficient manner and the report forwarded to A.D.M.S.	
12 noon	Admitted 23 sick — To C. Cl. Sta. 8 — To 82nd F.A.G. (one of self = rifles "wound", pos: accidental) 1 — To Duty 5 — Remained 13. Report wanted on the state of affairs re MMG6 attacks — orders to have carts was brought by order of acting ADMS of Lt./Col. BOYD and details were Reports to Hqrs 80th Bgde. charge of reports on re. incidents of 80th Brigade	
— 8 12 noon	Admitted 2 (wounded) + 23 sick. To C.C. Sta. 1. To F. and 9 Amb:1 (Self in hand), To duty 3. Remained 63. No officer collected, but a car with an NCO + 4 Bearers had sent up before to Lt. Col. BOYD.	
— 9 12 noon	Admitted 1 (wounded) + 22 sick. Remained 62. Men may sick to Rest Sta. 5, To Duty 22. Remained 62. Men may sick has high temps. Apparently we have 6 cases of mild influenza of a gastric type. We as yet have no [illegible] return reported.	M.O.6.h

Army Form C. 2118.

WAR DIARY
or
INTELLIGENCE SUMMARY.
(Erase heading not required.)

Instructions regarding War Diaries and Intelligence Summaries are contained in F.S. Regs., Part II and the Staff Manual respectively. Title pages will be prepared in manuscript.

Hour, Date, Place	Summary of Events and Information	Remarks and references to Appendices
ARMENTIERES		
June 10. 1 a.m.	Capt W.D. STURROCK reptd on return from leave.	
9 a.m.	Lt B. GOLDSMITH R.A.M.C. S.R. & Lt H.S. MILNE M.B., S.R. attached to 38th 3. Amb. reported for a six days course of instruction.	
12 noon	Adm: 2 wounded + 2 officers sick - To Cas. Cly. Sta. 15 To Bn: Rest Sta. 8. To Bns 16 - Died 1 - Remained 2 officers 140 -	
11. 30	Col. BROWNE, R.A.M.C. A.D.M.S. 2nd I. Division inspected the work of the 3rd Amb.	
12 noon	Admitted to arms std. 40 sick - To Car. Cl. Sta. 4 wounded 9-1 sick - To Bn: Rest Sta 8. To duty 1 Officer 8. Remained 33 Proceeded to Advanced Dressing Sta. Inspected arrangements and set readable order. W. CAROYD gave a very satisfactory report of the work & conduct of the detachment.	
4 p.m.	Re-arrangements of messing was made - the One Chaplain attny on sick - let officers and horse attendants, & the attached officers (38th 3. Amb) being brought into the mess.	H.G.G.W.

(73989) W.4141—463. 400,000. 9/14. H.&J.Ltd. Forms/C. 2118/10.

Army Form C. 2118.

WAR DIARY
or
INTELLIGENCE SUMMARY.
(Erase heading not required.)

Instructions regarding War Diaries and Intelligence Summaries are contained in F.S. Regs., Part II and the Staff Manual respectively. Title pages will be prepared in manuscript.

Hour, Date, Place	Summary of Events and Information	Remarks and references to Appendices
ARMENTIERES		
June 12. 12 noon	Arrivals 2 wounded & 5 sick. To Cas. Cly. Sta. 2 wounded and 2 sick. To Div: Rest Sta. 9 - To 82nd F.Amb. 1. (Reg. - sick?) To Duty 2. Remained 25.	
	Staff arranged for g.t. F.Amb.6: own H.Q. at ERQUINGHEM to take up Station. Own time on the Day of Dec.	
13. 11 a.m.	The D.D.M.S. 3rd Corps (Col. Bruce Skinner) inspects the Hospital Officers' tent: Rooms.	
12. noon.	Divine Service was celebrated in the Theatre at 11.30 a.m.	
	Activities 10 wounded 4 H. sick. Sent to Cas. Cly. Sta. 1 wounded + 2 sick. to Div: Rest Sta. 4. to duty 7. Remained 1 officer + 28.	
14. 12 noon.	Arrivals 4 wounded 1 officer + 25 sick. To Cas. Cly. Sta. 1 wounded 1 Sick. To Officers' Conv. Home 1 officer. To Duty 2. Remained 48.	
	Capt. Stanrock obtained from plate-0 some account of the source from which far-firing was obtained to the trenches on which On a votre it was forwarded. The statement obtained was forwarded to A.D.M.S.	
15. 12 noon	Arrivals 6 attacked 10 sick. To Cas. Cly. Sta. 1 wounded + 2 sick. To Div: Rest Sta. 6. Remained 23.	HAGM

Army Form C. 2118.

WAR DIARY
or
INTELLIGENCE SUMMARY.
(Erase heading not required.)

Instructions regarding War Diaries and Intelligence Summaries are contained in F.S. Regs., Part II and the Staff Manual respectively. Title pages will be prepared in manuscript.

Hour, Date, Place		Summary of Events and Information	Remarks and references to Appendices
ARMENTIERES			
June 15	4 p.m.	Among enemy shells fell close to the Ecole. None appeared to be of large calibre. None dropped near Explosr.	
16	6 p.m.	Lieut GOLDSMITH M'LURE & Lieuts D. MGARTH SDE to I Amb	
	9 a.m.	Lieuts: D.M. MORISON M.G., H.L.MANN & Lieut. THORN H.J. POL: HILL reported for duty as attached to this unit -	
	12 noon	Adm: 6 wounded + 2 officers + 9 sick - Sent to Cas. Clg. St. 3 sick. Do Div. Rec. St. 5. Do duty: 1. Remained 2 officers + 49.	
	8.30	Lt: MORISON M'MANN reported at Adv. Dr. St. and visited the ad'osts. Inspected the Adv. Dr. St. & carts in fosses in front. Inspected Transport Section & Head Quarters & not	
	10.30	Satisfactory. Admitted 1 officer + 3 wounded, 14 sick. Sent to Cas. Clg. St. 1 officer + 3 wounded, + 2 sick. Do Div. Rec. St. 12. Do duty 5. Remd: 2 officers + 44	
18	12 noon	Adm: 5 wounded + 15 sick. Do Cas. Clg. St.: 3 wounded + 2 sick Do Div. Rec. St.: 6. Do duty 3. Remained. 2 officers + 50 The Town Major called round the Ecole as to know from present billets	H.Q.G.H.

Army Form C. 2118.

WAR DIARY
or
INTELLIGENCE SUMMARY.
(Erase heading not required.)

Instructions regarding War Diaries and Intelligence Summaries are contained in F.S. Regs., Part II and the Staff Manual respectively. Title pages will be prepared in manuscript.

Hour, Date, Place	Summary of Events and Information	Remarks and references to Appendices
ARMENTIERES		
June 19 12 noon	Saw the Town Major & billet. The Mair was not at home. Subsequently received memo from Town Major saying that we were to leave at or on Monday. Sent strong protest by memo to A.D.M.S. who replied that he for one at once duty officer we were.	
	This took a second batch of NCOs men proceeded on leave to England — 8 in all.	
	Adm: 1 Officer(S) & 6 sick. To Cas. Clg. Sta; 2 found: 1 Sgt. to Gu	
	Recr. Sta. 1 (off Sgts)(?)(to Eng.) 2 Remained 1 off: 48	
	Divine Service was to-day 7 v. 11.30 a.m.	
20 12 noon	Adm: 4 obtruied 4 the sick. To Cas. Clg. Sta: 2 obtruied. 1 sick. To Gu. Recr. Sta. 4 to Bas 2. Remained 1 Officer	
	+53.	
21	Lt. Col. GODDARD. O.C. 38th F. Amb. arrived to inspect attach- ment. He rode the adv. dressing stn. wagons & foot a-coming.	HGGM
	Adm. 3 attained 1 sick. To Cas. Clg. Sta: 2 o: 4 sick. To Gu. Recr. Sta. 8 to Bas 2. Remained 1 Officer 150 men.	

Army Form C. 2118.

WAR DIARY
or
INTELLIGENCE SUMMARY.
(Erase heading not required.)

Instructions regarding War Diaries and Intelligence Summaries are contained in F.S. Regs., Part II and the Staff Manual respectively. Title pages will be prepared in manuscript.

Hour, Date, Place		Summary of Events and Information	Remarks and references to Appendices
ARMENTIERES			
June 21	8 p.m.	Lt Col GODDARD & Lt MORISON, MANN, and POLHILL with some NCO's who had also been attacked, returned for instructional purposes returned their unit.	
22	8.30 p.m.	Visited the Adv. Dr. St. & the Regtl Aid Post of 3rd KRRC.	
	12 noon	Adm: 2 wounded with sick. To Cas. Clg. St.: 1 wounded & 8 Sick	
		To Div. Recr. St: 5. To duty 4. Rmd: 1 off. + 53.	
	4.30 p.m.	Lieuts: C.J. Dillon-Kelly and G.D. SHANN of the 3rd Fd Amb Ambulance reported as attached for instructional purposes. Did then came 3 NCO's & 4 men. Three officers proceeded of the tanks proceeded to the same 3 to the Adv. Dr. St. Lt. Y. 2nd Aid post.	
23	12 noon	Adm: 6 wounded 1 Officer & 9 sick. To Cas. Clg. St.: 1 wounded	
		+ 3. To Div. Recr. St: 11. To duty 2. Remained 2 officers and 57.	
24	9 a.m.	Lt DILLON-KELLY and SHANN returned to duty with their unit.	
	12 noon	Admitted 2 wounded & 17 sick. To Cas. Clg. St: 1 wounded & 2 sick.	
		To Div. Recr. St: 7. To duty 5. Remained 2 officers + 59.	
		Total number evacuated to Cas. Clg. St for 7 days: 12 wounded	HGGM
		+ 16 sick.	

WAR DIARY or INTELLIGENCE SUMMARY

Army Form C. 2118.

(Erase heading not required.)

Instructions regarding War Diaries and Intelligence Summaries are contained in F.S. Regs., Part II and the Staff Manual respectively. Title pages will be prepared in manuscript.

Hour, Date, Place	Summary of Events and Information	Remarks and references to Appendices
ARMENTIERES		
June 25 9 noon	Adm; 3 wounded + 1 off. + 18 sick. To Cas. Cly. St. 4 ovac sick. 1 off. + 14 sick. Do Div. Rest St. 4. Remained 66.	
— 26 11.30 a.m.	Lt J.S.R. BOYD proceeded to England on 6 days' leave. Capt. Lt. C.A. BOYD R.A.M.C. with a view of transferring to Brigade H.Qs and attached to his present the charge of men of 8ot. Bgd. arranged together as adviser in HOOPLINES side show sanitaire to be used and in addition a post at (Hoglag) "Ration Dam". M.O. of R.S.L.I. was to effect return home of the wounded so. Subsequently saw A.D.M.S. who approved the proposed arrangement. Adm.; 1 officer + 6 sick. To Cas. Cly. St. 2 wounded + 1 off. + 5 sick. To Div. Rest St. 10. To Duty 2. 1 man died of wounds. Remained 2 officers + 61. Divine Service was held at the usual hour.	
— 27 11.30 a.m.	Lt. BELL (att. R.S.L.I.) came to see me. He stated that "Ration Dam" post in(?) noted close at hand. After that probably another day's musing. M.O. on R. of Bgd. to report there on 7th. Sept. To Div. Rest. St. 6. 81st D.M.S. for left. Note to O.C. 81st D.M.S. in these terms	A.D.M.S.

Army Form C. 2118.

WAR DIARY
or
INTELLIGENCE SUMMARY.
(Erase heading not required.)

ARMENTIERES

Hour, Date, Place	Summary of Events and Information	Remarks and references to Appendices
June 27 12 noon	Adm 4 wounded + 8 sick - To C.C. Cy. Stn 2 w: + 6 sick. To Div. Rest Stn 13 - To 82nd O Amb: ("SS9"="infants") 2 - To duty 5. Remained 2 officers + 45.	
28 10.30 a.m.	D.D.M.S. 3rd Army Corps paid us the hospital a visit.	
12 noon	Admitted 2 wounded + 4 sick - To C.C.Cy Stn 1 wounded. To Div. Rest Stn: 5. Remained 55.	
29	Somewhat quieter under the four distinct damage than usual. 3 NCOs were killed ½ another ½ wounded and infantry attached ½ another. They had post amnesty called the "Ferme du Bizet" was much trying to continuous shelling. They also fired known as "SPECIAL" will be send to the HOSPICES sch On the CHAPELLE sick "Roten Sam" continued to be used.	
12 noon	Admitted 7 wounded + 6 sick. To Cas: Cy. Stn. 8 wounded +13. To Div. Rest Stn 17. To duty 2. Remained 2 officers 40 -	NGGN

WAR DIARY
or
INTELLIGENCE SUMMARY.
(Erase heading not required.)

Army Form C. 2118.

Hour, Date, Place	Summary of Events and Information	Remarks and references to Appendices
ARMENTIERES June 30 12 noon	Adm: 2 wounded and 15 sick – To Cas. Cy. Et. 1 wounded, 12 sick – To Offrs Conv. Dépôt 1. To Div. Rest Stn. 1 – To A.T.S. 2. Remained 1 Officer and 45. The chief noticeable clinical features during the month was the occurrence of cases of abdominal & intestinal symptoms more after the than not on sudden seizure than the previous gastric condition. In addition we have had great evils & a large number of cases of "conjunctivitis" about which M.O's seem to hesitate to declare a part of hara[illegible]'s revisit. Apart from this the characteristics of a gastric type of influenza & the distinct hot weather malarial look have, in the distinct absence of the usual causes noted for Troops on these lines.	#G6M

121/6292

AMD

27th Division

121/6292

83rd Field Ambulance

Vol VII

July 15

Confidential.

83rd Field Ambulance R.A.M.C

War Diary

July, 1915.

Army Form C. 2118.

WAR DIARY
or
INTELLIGENCE SUMMARY.
(Erase heading not required.)

Instructions regarding War Diaries and Intelligence Summaries are contained in F.S. Regs., Part II. and the Staff Manual respectively. Title pages will be prepared in manuscript.

Hour, Date, Place	Summary of Events and Information	Remarks and references to Appendices
July 1 ARMENTIERES 12 noon	Adm: 1 wounded + 7 sick. To Cas. Cly. Hosp: 2 wounded + 3 sick. To Div: M.T.St: 4. To Office Cont Dept: 1. To B of S. Returned 38. Aeroplane over (many of French orchestra) was gun in during. Several shells during some execution for our convoy to the morning.	H.Q.M.
2 12 noon	Adm: 3 wounded + 12 sick. To Cas: Cly. Hosp: 4 wounded and 5 sick. To Div. Rest St: 5. To 82nd Brig. Amb S. (Brig): (Fcas): 1. To B of S 4. Returned 36. Lt. A.H. BREWER posted to take over as strong. Adm.ted 4 officers ret wounded and 43 sick. and 4 sick. To Div. Rest St: 3. To	
3 12 noon	Lty 5. Returned 36. Lt. J.S.F. BOYD posted on return from leave. Shelling was somewhat heated in the afternoon but appeared to cease as ascertained no military too was cast—to Asaby –	
4 12 noon	Adm: St: 2. To Cas: Cly. St: 10. + 1 sick. To Div. Rest St: 2. To B of S. Returned 45. Divine Service was held in the streets at the usual times –	

Army Form C. 2118.

WAR DIARY
or
INTELLIGENCE SUMMARY.
(Erase heading not required.)

Instructions regarding War Diaries and Intelligence Summaries are contained in F.S. Regs., Part II and the Staff Manual respectively. Title pages will be prepared in manuscript.

Hour, Date, Place	Summary of Events and Information	Remarks and references to Appendices
ARMENTIERES		
July 5 12 noon	Arrived 3 wounded & 13 sick. To Cas: Clg: Stn: 3 w. & 2 sick - Do Div: Rec: Stn: 9 Do July 6. Rcvd 1 off. & 41	ABM
2.30 p.m.	AOMS 2) a Division instructed the transport section. BABMS informed me that, as Lt RICE (attd 4th RB) would be away on leave in a few days, & Capt WILLIAMSON (attd 3D RWC) wanted to act BABMS during his absence or leave. it would be necessary for us to supply medical officers in their place. Lieut SOMMS & Lieut ALABASTER to proceed to the 4th attached, the other to function as troops in billets from time to time.	
12 noon	In the morning Lt SOMMS saw Lt RICE & arranged to take over the work of M.O. attd 4th RB on night of July 7th inst. Lt ALABASTER & Capt WILLIAMSON in 8th RB rough book is below on y.s. Adm: 7 wounded 42 sick. To Cas: Clg: Stn: 2 wounded 17 sick rd. Do Div: Rec: Stn: 6. Do Inf: H. & Sick officers 3. Remained 1 officer 143.	

— 6. —

WAR DIARY
or
INTELLIGENCE SUMMARY
(Erase heading not required.)

Army Form C. 2118.

Hour, Date, Place	Summary of Events and Information	Remarks and references to Appendices
ARMENTIERES (contin.)		
July 6.	The town was rather heavily shelled in the afternoon. No military casualties reported.	ABGh
12 noon	Admitted) 3 wounded and 14 sick. — 2o Cav: Cy. St: 3 wounded & sick. — 2o Div: Rec Stn: 4. — 2o Bgd. 1 off. w. Remainder 45.	
9 p.m.	Accompanied Lt SONNTAG to Ratio Farm. The stretcher Arranged with M SONNTAG that if it became unusable he should send it down & have got way of & both clearly. Any future stages offered. Subsequently it appeared that Dr RICE was unable to obtain leave yet so on the next day M SONNTAG reported, it was arranged that he should take on work as RMO of 2nd RRR from 9 a.m. 16th.	
8 — 12 noon	Admitted) 3 wounded and 1m sick. 2o Cav: Cy St: 3 w; and 1 sick. 2o Div: Rec Stn: 8. Remainder 44.	
2.30 pm	ADMS 2nd Army Corps inspected Hospital Officers Corps Home.	
9 — 12 noon	Admitted) 1 wounded & 8 sick. 2o Cav: Cy St: 3½: 4 3 sick. 2o Div: Rec Stn: 7. 2o Bgdy. 1 Mc Died of Remainder 36.	

Army Form C. 2118.

WAR DIARY
or
INTELLIGENCE SUMMARY.
(Erase heading not required.)

Instructions regarding War Diaries and Intelligence Summaries are contained in F.S. Regs., Part II and the Staff Manual respectively. Title pages will be prepared in manuscript.

Hour, Date, Place	Summary of Events and Information	Remarks and references to Appendices
ARMENTIERES July 3	Altks. for Commanders Declaration read before the "en-employed object of Corps. H. MORSE." to said to have obeyed. been the for 3 under assistance in emergency. Fall hits "A Dets" to maintenance of discipline, and his influence has been wholly for good". Several shots - affray of hype calibre - were thrown into the town.	AAG h
6 p.m.		
— 10. 11.30 a.m.	ADMS inspected motor ears attacked guns tanks goodworks ten.	
— 11. 7 p.m.	On review of private memoirs of past of unit to N. of Rain Lys. 2 N.C.Os + 5 men. Castes have this afternoon, with furniture of D.A.Q.M.S. taken furniture of Hollebeke Farm, Striker away. B. 20. c. (Franc. Sheet 36. ¼ worn). Admitted 13 sick + 5 wounded. T.C.C.H. 2w + 3.S. To 2. R.S. 12.S. To duty + 2 sick. Remaining 29. Major H MACKENZIE left for England on leave.	W.T.J.

(73989) W4141—463. 400,000. 9/14. H.&J.Ltd. Forms/C. 2118/10.

Army Form C. 2118.

WAR DIARY
or
INTELLIGENCE SUMMARY.
(Erase heading not required.)

Instructions regarding War Diaries and Intelligence Summaries are contained in F.S. Regs., Part II. and the Staff Manual respectively. Title pages will be prepared in manuscript.

Hour, Date, Place	Summary of Events and Information	Remarks and references to Appendices
ARMENTIERES.		WTS
July 12. 12 noon.	Lt. PYTER reported on return from leave. Admitted 3 w. & 16 sick. To C.C.H. 5 w. & 6 s. To I.R.S. 8 sick. To duty 2 sick. Remaining 27.	
July 13. 5.30 p.m.	Admitted 5 w. & 13 s. To C.C.H. 3 w. & 13 s. To I.R.S. 3 sick. To duty 4 sick. To Officers Convalescent Depot 1. Remaining 29. On confidential orders received last evening, the party at Hilltype farm was notified this morning; on further orders at noon today the same party was sent back to the farm & again took possession of it. Visited the farm yesterday with Lt. DEVENALD & found the position & accommodation very good.	
July 14. 11.30 A.M.	At 10 A.M. took over medical charge of 82nd Brigade in addition to 80th; patients from 82nd F! Amb. were transferred to Ecole. Lt. C.A. BOYD notifies that drivers during stables were to deal with 82nd Brigade in addition. 82nd F! Amb. moved out of the town this morning.	

(73989) W4141—463. 400,000. 9/14. H.&J.Ltd. Forms/C. 2118/10.

Army Form C. 2118.

WAR DIARY
or
INTELLIGENCE SUMMARY.
(Erase heading not required.)

Instructions regarding War Diaries and Intelligence Summaries are contained in F.S. Regs., Part II. and the Staff Manual respectively. Title pages will be prepared in manuscript.

Hour, Date, Place	Summary of Events and Information	Remarks and references to Appendices
ARMENTIÈRES		VII
July 14. 12 nn.	Admitted. 3 w. + 17 s. To C.C.H. 3 w. + 10 s. To S.R.S. 8 sick. T. to dy. 3 sick. Remaining 25.	
7 p.m.	The Town was extensively shelled from 10.30 am — 1 p.m. Apparently no few casualties. 1 orderly + 3 water drawn had to remain during shelling, & extra tiring party; advance dressing station, & extra work being probable. Capt A.N. MAYBURY from 26th F.A. Ambce. reported for duty.	
July 15. 12 nn.	Admitted. 7 w. + 9 s. from 82nd Fd Ambce. + 3 w. + 14 s. total 10 w. + 23 s. T. C.C.H. 3 w + s s. To S.R.S. 10 s To duty. 4 s. Sick 1. Remaining 35. Forwarded + recommended Capt MAYBURY's application to return to his own unit.	
6 p.m.	Moved, in the afternoon, all C section wagons, pack + saddle, & wheelers stores & some more personnel, to HOUSE EPPS FARM.	
July 16. 12 nn.	Admitted 11 w. + 34 s. To C.C.H. 9 w. + 6 s. To D.R.S. 2 w. + 21 s. To 82nd Fd Ambce. 7 w. + 15 s. To Duty 1 s. Sick 1 w. Remaining 18.	

WAR DIARY
or
INTELLIGENCE SUMMARY
(Erase heading not required.)

Army Form C. 2118

Instructions regarding War Diaries and Intelligence Summaries are contained in F.S. Regs., Part II. and the Staff Manual respectively. Title Pages will be prepared in manuscript.

Place	Date	Hour	Summary of Events and Information	Remarks and references to Appendices
ARMENTIÈRES	July 16	6 p.m.	At 4.30 p.m. met Lt ALABASTER with remainder C. Section to form, with orders to put up during station. Lt PYPER to take charge of patients. Lt DEVONALD in command of walking party. Lt PYPER with orders to get into touch with M.O.i. 8th Brigade in their new areas. Handed over Officers convalescent depôt to 36th Fd Amb.	WDI
"	July 17	2 p.m.	Visits from in morning, & found all work satisfactorily accomplished. Admitted 5 w. & 22 S. To C.C.H. 5 w & 15 S.; to D.R.S. 7 S. To duty 2. Remaining 16.	
"	July 18	12 n'n	Handed over Ecole & billet to 3rd Northumbrian Fd Amb, 50th Div. Moved off at 10 a.m. Arrived Hollebeke 11.3. Have been transferred to 1st Army. Admitted 19 S. To C.C.H. 9 S.; to D.R.S. 6 S. Remaining 20.	
FERME HOLLEBEKE ARMENTIÈRES	July 19	12 noon	Lt. J. S. K. BOYD, 1st Vt, 2 L. Corporals & 16 men took on Divisional duties from 19th Fd Amb, all having received instruction this day before. Admitted 24 S. Remaining 44. Returns is now due 9 a.m. in place of 12 noon.	
"	July 20	9 a.m. 8.30 a.m.	Lt. SONNTAG, with 1 orderly & motor ambulance, went to brevet school at La Gorgnette to take on for day. Major A/G Mackenzie reported on return from leave.	HGM
"	21	9 a.m.	Adm: 19 sick. To Cas: Cly. St. 12. To duty: Rest. Stn 2. Remained 34. Inspected the camp in detail. Engl.g.3 is in satisfactory order & reflects credit on the org. officer shown resp.: 5 Capt STORROCK, the Transport Officer, and the Quartermaster Pacheler a still in Sufferuil hospital Boulogne –	

1875 Wt. W593/826 1,000,000 4/15 J.B.C. & A. A.D.S.S./Forms/C. 2118.

WAR DIARY
or
INTELLIGENCE SUMMARY

Army Form C. 2118

(Erase heading not required.)

Instructions regarding War Diaries and Intelligence Summaries are contained in F.S. Regs., Part II. and the Staff Manual respectively. Title Pages will be prepared in manuscript.

Place	Date	Hour	Summary of Events and Information	Remarks and references to Appendices
3rd me HOLLEBEKE A-ARMENTIERES	July 21	11 a.m.	The ADMS and DADMS rode to billets.	HQQM
	22	9 a.m.	Admitted 11 sick. 2 Cas. Cly. Sta. 5. 2 Div. Rest Sta: 9. 2 Div: 2. Rnd: 29.	
		4 p.m.	Maj. Gen: G.F. MILNE C.B., D.S.O. accompanied by the ADMS inspected the Camp, beg Welfare recreation rooms etc., which the General had own the 3 Aust since his recent appointment as G.B.C. 2) A-Division.	
		5.30 p.m.	The DDMS 2nd Army accompanied by the DDMS 3rd Army Corps inspected the Camp. Some successful boring competitions were held in Camp.	
	23	9 a.m.	Heavy cannonading at some distance was heard & continued all the evening and continued into the night. Admitted 10 sick. 2 Cas. Cly. Sta: 4. 2 Div: Rest Sta: 12. 2 Div: 2 Remainder 21.	
		2.30 p.m.	Inspected the 2) the Divl Baths at EQUVINGHEM under control of MJ SK(?) man met (?) with to completion of the arrangements for washing returns of men.	
		5.30 p.m.	Received orders from ADMS 2 Divl to shew for (Infantry) service with 3rd	
			Bye R.S.A. Instructors Lt. ALABASTER Expert for duty.	
	24	9 a.m.	Admitted 14 sick. 2 Cas. Cly. Sta: 9 (incl. 4 till wom. khaki) Remained 26. Under orders from ADMS It SONNING again reported for duty at Bombfactory.	
	25	9 a.m.	Admitted 13 sick. 2 Divl. Cly. Sta: 1. 2 Divl Rest Sta: 1. 2 Divl: 2. 3. Remained 28. The unit attended & Divl Service at billets of 4th R.B.	
		10 a.m.	DADMS brought interesting information of the attendance of Guinea worm among troops - two cases had been noted among men of Highland Lt. Brigade lately returned from the East. date July 24. dia A.P.L. DEVONALD Gazetted Captain.	

WAR DIARY
or
INTELLIGENCE SUMMARY
(Erase heading not required.)

Army Form C. 2118

Instructions regarding War Diaries and Intelligence Summaries are contained in F.S. Regs., Part II. and the Staff Manual respectively. Title Pages will be prepared in manuscript.

Place	Date	Hour	Summary of Events and Information	Remarks and references to Appendices
ROLLEBEQUE FARM ARMENTIERES	July 26	9 a.m.	Admitted 7 sick. To Las: Cly. Sta: 4. To Div: Rest Sta 9. To Bng 1. Remained 21.	AGM
		1 p.m.	R'cvied orders from ADMS to detail one officer to relieve Lt: Rice M.O. at 1/1 HLB. R.B- on leave from 2nd Bn. Inst: Detailed Lt. Robinson which referential work at Bomb School was in abeyance.	
		4 p.m.	Visit J.C. MARRIOVE from 2/1 South Midland 3. Amb: reports no taken on strength until other war Officers of -	
	27	5 p.m.	Capt ASHBURY under orders appointed 2646 3. Amb - His place was taken by 2 Lieut: HARLOW. but the officer was with Group Joy.	
	27	9 a.m.	Admitted 14 sick - To Las: Cly Sta. 0. To Div. Rest Sta 7. Remained 28. Total sick - C.C.S. for 7 days 35 - Average 5 per diem - Anopheles did a good deal of reconnaissance. Three of the parties were more child out apparent without result. Heavy fire of casting fire on the front was observed in the ground heard, some snipers got a special good shot he was begun with a view to a portage of stay. The Premier promise before the stops in sets the the our plans.	
	28	9 a.m.	Admitted 2 officer + 1 man. To Cas: Cly Sta: 7. To Div: Rest Sta: 5. Remained 2 officer	
		10 a.m.	Pursuant to orders D.G. No. 762/6, JMS 23 Army No. 146/1, the following promotions are announced -
			To be Captains: Lieut. A.H. BREWER, Dvrfd. Capt. A.E.L. DEVONALD, Lieut. J.C. PYPER M.B. - dates April 1 1915 - Capt Pyper's name appears in today's gazette -	

WAR DIARY
or
INTELLIGENCE SUMMARY
(Erase heading not required.)

Army Form C. 2118

Instructions regarding War Diaries and Intelligence Summaries are contained in F.S. Regs., Part II. and the Staff Manual respectively. Title Pages will be prepared in manuscript.

Place	Date	Hour	Summary of Events and Information	Remarks and references to Appendices
MOUSEBERGE FARM ARMENTIERES	July 29	9 a.m.	Admitted 10 sick. To Cas. Cy. Sta. 4. To Div. Rest Sta. 2 Officers no. Pm. 3: 21. Lt. J.C.F. BOYD certified a temp: unfit store nature was detained in Camp. Capt PIPER was attached to take over the management of the Divisional Baths. Considerable progress had been made with the sanitary improvements and the litching in the last 24 hours. The Sgt Major whilst proceeding to the Baths with Capt PIPER collided with 2 metal horses of 1st Bn. Cam. 65 as a result of which one horse broke his leg and had to be shot. Sgt Major Capt PIPER & the driver of the car & Private Sept statements regarding the matter. 6 BOMBS exercised rifle & machine gun fire with Vickers Instant Cammans, overhead and started fire in the night.	AGGM
	−30	9 a.m.	Admitted 14 sick. To Cas. Cy. Sta. 3. To Div. Rest Sta. 5. To Div. Sta. 1. Pm. 3:26.	
	−31	9 a.m.	Admitted. To Cas. Cy. Sta. 6. To Div. Rest Sta. 3. To Div. Bag 2. Pm. 3: 20.	
		5 p.m.	Major CHENERY Surrey Yeomany off/py.gd. Arrived in the Transport Section for the first days but brought horses and harness.	
		6 p.m.	ADMS & BADMS visited the camp. ADMS saw some patients admitted as unfit for service and inspected the new sanitary arrangements. BADMS conferred with Off. STURROCK ARMO's of 2nd Brigade on questions of trench hygiene.	

27th Division

121/6598

83rd Field Ambulance, R.A.M.C.

Confidential

War Diary.
August, 1915.

Vol VIII

WAR DIARY or INTELLIGENCE SUMMARY

Army Form C. 2118

Place	Date 1915	Hour	Summary of Events and Information	Remarks and references to Appendices
HOUPLINES FARM ARMENTIÈRES	Aug 1	9 a.m.	Admitted 10 sick. Discharged Cpl St. 4. To Div. Rest Sta. 4. To Duty 1. Remained 21.	H.G.M.
		11 a.m.	Lts. I. A. B. & Hts. D. Ch. Parade at H.Qs 4th R.B.	
			This was the first really hot day since end of June.	
	2	9 a.m.	Admitted 1 wounded r6 sick. Discharged Cpl. St. 1 wounded r6 sick (nebula). To Bn. Hosp. Rest Sta. 2. To duty 1. Remained 16.	
		3 p.m.	D.D.M.S. H.3 Army Corps inspected billets and horse transport lines.	
	3	8 a.m.	Capt. PYPER with NCO + 8 men proceeded to Adv. Dr. Sta. CHAPELLE D'ARMENTIÈRES and	
			on for the 81st.	
	9 a.m.	Capt. STURROCK, Lt. SONTAG and C Section personnel regimental proceeded to ERQUINGHEM and there collected Divisional HQs, taking over from 81st F.A. Subsequently Sgt STURROCK took reports that matters were going smoothly.	
			Adm. 2 officers + 20 sick. To Cas. Cl. Sta. 3. To Div. Rest Sta. 1 off. 4. Remained 1 off. 26.	
			Satisfying matches obtained and a traces of skins spread over the land.	
	4	7 a.m.	Lt. C. A. BOYD sports on return from leave.	
		9 a.m.	Adm. 2 wounded + 13 sick. To Cas. Cl. Sta. 2 wounded + 4 off. + 9 sick. To Div. Rest Sta. 4. To Duty 3. Remained 23.	
		12 noon	To the C. Section HQs, billet strafed and the wounded officers station at CHAPELLE D'ARMENTIÈRES. Baths were all arranged. Rather more sick casualties than are anticipated have come in. Wounded	
			casualties are still few.	
	5	9 a.m.	Admitted C. S. Lieut. D. Sr. admitted 3 wounded + 18 sick. To Cas. Cl. St. wounded + 5 sick. To Div. Rest Sta. 2 Remained 35.	
		2 p.m.	Proceeded direct to Adv. Br. Sta. There with Capt. PYPER to review aid posts. (i) KSLI (ii) PPCLI (iii) 3d Bn. KRRC. All are of the nature of dugouts. This situation is convenient	

Army Form C. 2118

WAR DIARY
or
INTELLIGENCE SUMMARY
(Erase heading not required.)

Instructions regarding War Diaries and Intelligence Summaries are contained in F. S. Regs., Part II. and the Staff Manual respectively. Title Pages will be prepared in manuscript.

Place	Date 1915	Hour	Summary of Events and Information	Remarks and references to Appendices
ROLLEBEQUE FARM ARMENTIERES	Aug 5		and conditions be improved. In the present state of operations they ought to be dealt with. This could be carried on in the space between the old buildings. If many cases had to be dealt with this could be carried on in the space between the stretcher cases down communication trenches remains. Capt WILLIAMSON (3rd NRFC) is preparing a second dug out in a well chosen spot. From his advanced post only, by night, a wheeled stretcher can be used with advantage. Up to now two bearer RMO's, as it cannot be brought in are not the roads reached. Capt WILLIAMSON has also the advantage of being able to bring in water carts up to his right Hqs Bridge where to take advantage of it successful cases while the water is chlorinated. In other case the water carts have to wait at the foot of the communication trenches. The sanitary condition of the Brigade area seems to be satisfactory.	44 9m
		5 p.m.	Major G.H. FLINT reported for temporary attachment to this unit.	
			Remains 30. Achilles 1 wounded 41 sick. Do. Cav. Clg. Sta. 4 wounded 16 sick. Do. Do. Rest Sta. 6. 2. 3. 51.	
	6	9 a.m.	Heavy gunfire at no great distance heard. Continued some hours.	
		10 p.m.	Morning papers of 6th inst. contained official announcement from Berlin of the occupation of WARSAW by the Russians & the occupation of the city by German Troops.	
	7	9 a.m.	Office HQ. Do. Cas. 2. Admitted 2 wounded + 23 sick. Do. Cav. Clg. Sta. 2 or 3 d. 49 sick (appx) Do. Div. Rest Sta. Remain 39.	
		10 a.m.	Major HARVEY Quartermaster (61st 9 Amb) at the bed for information.	
	8	9 a.m.	Admitted 8 wounded + 12 sick. Do. Cav. Clg. Sta. 8 wnd + 7 sick. Do. Div. Rest Sta. 15.	
		11.30 —	Divine Service was held in the Transport field.	
	9	4 a.m.	An extremely heavy bombardment began & continued until 7. Our guns appeared to be taking the lead.	

WAR DIARY
or
INTELLIGENCE SUMMARY
(Erase heading not required.)

Army Form C. 2118

Instructions regarding War Diaries and Intelligence Summaries are contained in F. S. Regs., Part II. and the Staff Manual respectively. Title Pages will be prepared in manuscript.

Place	Date 1915	Hour	Summary of Events and Information	Remarks and references to Appendices
HOLLEBEQUE FARM ARMENTIERES	Aug 9 (contd)	9 a.m.	Adm: 1 wounded +12 sick. To Cas: Cy Sta 8.- To Div: Rest Sta: 4. To det 3. Remained 23.- Weather throughout the day was very hot.	A4GM
			The horses the so. Guard - but there are none of correspondent schemes -	
		9 a.m.	Adm: 3 wounded +1 officer +21 sick. - To Cas: Cy. Sta: 3 off 98 +1 officer + 4 sick. To Div: Rest Sta: 4. To duty 2. Remained 34.	
		3 p.m.	ADMS BATHS 9) to Division visited the Camp. AVERAGE daily wastage of sick (incl. officers) 5.5 (10 days). Brown was got to the reestablishment of stairs for house and the sinking of a well.	
	-11	9 a.m.	Adm: 1 wounded + 1 officer and 21 sick. To Cac: Cy. Sta: 1 wounded + 7 sick. To Div: Rest Sta: 1 officer +22. Rmng: 25.	
			BATHS informed me that there was no probability of bricks being issued by the R.E. for house stabilyt until we were informed of the recognition of arrangement later for winter quarter.	
		6 p.m.	Our tradings good coart arranged by 81ST Field Amb: at GREENWERCR at which some of the unit assisted.	
	-12	9 a.m.	Adm: 5 wounded + 1 officer +21 sick. To Cas: Cy. Sta: 5 wd 98 +1 officer + 5. To Div: Rest Sta 9. To duty 3. Remaining 29.	
		5 p.m.	ADMS +DDMS visited the Camp. Informed that according to present arrangements the unit would probably be called upon to use as winter quarter HOLLEBEQUE FARM, The Transport Barn at present occupied by 2) Fd. Amb: 3 Amb: Workshops.	
	-13	3 a.m.	A sharp rifle explosion at the gun of trench close at hand. Which did not suggest a bursting shell or proximity of a rifle explosion but sound	

Army Form C. 2118

WAR DIARY
or
INTELLIGENCE SUMMARY
(Erase heading not required.)

Instructions regarding War Diaries and Intelligence Summaries are contained in F.S. Regs., Part II. and the Staff Manual respectively. Title Pages will be prepared in manuscript.

Place	Date	Hour	Summary of Events and Information	Remarks and references to Appendices
FARM HOLLEBEQUE ARMENTIERES (en r)	Aug 13	9.a.m	Admitted 1 wounded + 11 sick. To Cas: Clg: Stn: 1 wounded + 3 sick. To Div: Rest Stn: 5. Remaining 28 -	A 44 m
		9.30 -	Inspected the accommodation at the 3 farms in the neighbourhood. The Barn + the Transport farm offer no slender facilities for billeting, and, so if the barns & granaries were taken over, we should have to tie floor through to the going refuse. At the workshops Barn there is much better accommodation - Billets 100 - 120 men could be housed there. There is good clean dry ground for men & ambulance waggons. Subsequently was informed by D.A.D.M.S. that it was of doubtful if any of them billets could be located as entire question.	
		3 pm	A/Cpt visited the Camp in company with A.D.M.S. and inspected the Sanitary arrangements. Adm: 1 wounded + 22 - C Sn: 1 wounded + 4 - Div: Rest Stn: 4. Evac: 2. Remaining 41-	
	-14	9 a.m	Accompanied Major WILLAN, Capt HUSTON, Lt Cmdr AEGGH MATAHIS. I visited the site of Amb: at DOU- LIEU. On the way I stopped at 61st Gen Hos: at STEENVOORDE to arrange details of transfer of dental cases.	
		3 pm		
	-15	9 a.m	Admitted 2 officer + 1 wounded and 15 sick. To Cas: Clg: Stn: 2 off + 1 wound and 4 sick. To Div: Rest Stn: 1. To Gen S.g. Remaining 36.	
		3 p.m	Visited Baths - verified that the arrangements were if there was any provision for constant complaints to be sufficient in case of men being at Bath. The OC las been were in clothes taken off. Men's had found a knapsack for more than two form which were not items where? Doctor Day Knapsack for more than two form which were not items where? Typical in Natural.	

WAR DIARY or INTELLIGENCE SUMMARY

Army Form C. 2118

Place	Date	Hour	Summary of Events and Information	Remarks and references to Appendices
BELLEVUE FARM HINGETTES	Aug 16	9.a.m. Bty: 1) 9.a.m.	Adm: 1 off wounded, 413 sick. To Cas: Cy Sta: 1 off add 12 sick. To Bn Prov Sta: 9 - To Bn Sig: 8 - Ring 30 81st Bgd: kknd 82nd to Tonkers. To tr: Armng: 1 in Tonkers 2 weeks longer - Adm: 1 off + 3 wounded, 146 sick. To Cas: Cy Sta: 1 off + 3 wounded - + 3 sick - To Bn: Prov St: 3. To Bn Sig: 7 - Remaining 33 - After a fine morning clouds came up with an accompaniment of thunder lightning & heavy downpour began. This subsequent changed to a hailstorm of great violence the hailstones being of considerably more than average size. He had ceased & was succeeded by rain about torrential in volume. Sand bag clay been too badly -	HQ Gd
		5.30 p.m.	ADMS visited Camp. Informed that it was of improbable that the present billets could be used during the two months. A cable began - but stopped at end of day from instructions about occupation of billets (T.SONNIAS)	
		-18 9.a.m.	Adm: 1 off, 4th sick - To Cas: Cy St:) Sick - To Bn: Prov St: 6 - To Bn Sig: 4. Ring: 1 Off: 30 - Lt. MARKLOVE with NCO & 12 rifles forms re' to billets arm & returns from Bgd will 4th Bn APRC. Capt DEVONALD (T.O) who had been sick some days will	
		9.30 - 10.15 -	to C.O. Sta: MERVILLE. The time of 74 (Recon) Bgy. Ont in no news of death or situation of Lt-Col. G.A. ROSELL. formerly O.C. tr & inst - This that had been reported for some weeks.	

1875   Wt. W593/826 1,000,000 4/15 J.B.C. & A. A.D.S.S./Forms/C. 2118.

WAR DIARY
or
INTELLIGENCE SUMMARY
(Erase heading not required.)

Army Form C. 21

Place	Date	Hour	Summary of Events and Information	Remarks and references to Appendices
HALLEBAST FARM ARMENTIERS	Aug. 18		A plan of the thing suggested by Col. Broome ADMS 27 a Div. Experimented with. Dirs are placed upside down. Lid buried on soft ground. This gave filled with earth. The bottom of tin (now top) is left bare surface of ground. Spaces between tins are filled in with earth. This is light sand above tinted surface. The scheme seems to be promising provided. A piece of ground tested (area of 5'9" × 2'7") is occupied to-morrow about 2 horse but (i) collection of tin motors some delay; (ii) after practice it may be assumed that the tins will be considerably reduced. Semi diagrammatic sketch.	HQm
		5 p.m.	Lt MARKLOVE made a fair hopeful report in operation in [?] Dr. St. at SADUINGHEM Sendr. Dr. St. at CHAPELLE D'ARMEN; TIERES. Everything seems suitable.	
	19	9 a.m	Lt. MARKLOVE took temp. charge of transport vice Capt OSTERALD absent sick. ADM III. 3 wounded 2 officers 1 sick. To Cae. Clg. Stn. 3 ORs + 1 off + 6 sick. 2 other ranks Stn. 1 off + 8. Army R.S.	
		2.30 p.m.	Inspected hospital billets with Lt. MARKLOVE, Lt tom r KEOGH. 7 p.m. Officers from billets. Sergeants Canteen tea with B.A.D.M.S. & raised further additional motor quarters house opening all stalls. Put A.Th.28 Lt. MARKLOVE trouble with Coal. On temp. was inspected by ADMS, DADMS bringing KAYLIS Div. mother.	
	20	9 a.m.	ADM. 1 off wound 2 + 15 Field. 2 Cae. Cl. St. 0. To Div. Rest St. 6. 1 officer died of bounds. Remaining 35. Large number of sick cases are out to Div. Rest St.	

WAR DIARY
or
INTELLIGENCE SUMMARY

Army Form C. 2118

Place	Date	Hour	Summary of Events and Information	Remarks and references to Appendices
FARM HAZEBROUCK HAZEBROUCK	Aug 22	9 a.m.	Admitted 2 wounded + 19 sick. To Cas: Cy: Sta: 12 + 6 sick. To Div: Rest Sta: 12. To Base (S.). Remaining 29.	AGGM
		10 a.m.	Conference at ADMS' office with APM 2) Or Div: a formation of first of M. Police Gr: Cassidi, ma: Emphasising the difficulties of dealing with the matter. The org. explained to had be came and that (i) most must use every endeavour to keep APM with all possible information. (ii) if in a mistake by police, men suffers from rev. disease, Major Ward (First 2AMB) called attention to an important point – the mistake of 3792.3 that took to a condition of ulcer should be sent back to Guy ADMS' said that information had been made to the base but without effect.	
		12 g.a.m.	Adm: 1 off. + 5 wounded, 14 sick. To Cas: Cy: Sta: 1 off. 14 wdd. 9 sick. To Div: R. Sta: 6. D.D. of wounds 1. To Aug 3 – Amy: 25	
		10 a.m.	Inspected Transport taken at 46 RAMC and combined Transf: billets + billets of 34 RAMC, with AB, 2nd NSH, 16 PC.11. Barber is in capital condition – all was apparently well in the later Sect: Section has to cook & trans & we do some transporting on repair lines. Works much has been done so far. Saline Service worked at 11.30 a.m. 16.30 p.m.	
	23	9 a.m.	Adm: 4 wounded, 1-2 officer 43 sick. To Cas: Cy: St: 4 wounded. To Div: Rest St: 2 off.	
		3 p.m.	30 sick. To Aug: 6. Any: 28. Officer was sent from BHQ of a study of a staff Hand Success in Ex Baltic.	
	24	9 a.m.	Adm: 1 off. 5 wounded, 175 sick. To Cas Cy Sta: 1 off. 11 wounded + 7 sick. To Div: Rest Sta: 8. To Base 5. Any: 23. Average Sick Wastage per Div. (at days) 4.6	

Army Form C. 2118

WAR DIARY
or
INTELLIGENCE SUMMARY
(Erase heading not required.)

Instructions regarding War Diaries and Intelligence Summaries are contained in F.S. Regs., Part II. and the Staff Manual respectively. Title Pages will be prepared in manuscript.

Place	Date	Hour	Summary of Events and Information	Remarks and references to Appendices
FARM MOLLEBEKE LARMONTMEERS	Aug '25	9 a.m.	Adm: 3 odd + 181 - Do Cas Clg Sta. 3 odd + 3 Sick - Do Div: Res Sta. 6 - Do Bag.S. Amazing 27 -	HQ A
		10.30 a.m	Our Sec'n to Bath. A Fortign and 9 other. Sound Sanmnn. On the way discovered a foot from RAMCs with Capt STORROCK -	
		2 p.m.	Completion of Dum-fect sections of various DADs held at ERQUINGHEM. Our Transport arrived but Stored around till this pgn.	
	26	9 a.m.	Lt. MABASTER arrived. 3rd C Bgde RFA struck off strength. Adm: 11 sick. Do Cas Clg Sta. 3. Do Div Res Sta. 2 Do Bag. 4. Amazing 29 - Weather became again very warm.	
	27	9 a.m.	Divn " 26/8/15 on place announcement of award of St. George (4th Class) Pte STAPLETON H. of (Russian) award of Adm: 5 odd + 4 sick Do Cas Clg: Sta. 5 odd + 4 sick. Do Bri: Res Sta 4 Do Bag.5. Amazing 35.	
	28	9 a.m.	Inaugurated a new system of checking men's kits and extra oil clothes of medical + CCS divisions. Adm: 2 odd + 1 off + 12 sick Do Cas: Clg. Sta: 2 odd + 1 off + 2 sick. Do Fld Res Sta. 6- Do Bag. Amazing 32	
		12 noon	Visited ERQUINGHEM + went up with Capt STORROCK to Adv. Dr. St. This is not now suitable the order. Left the BRASSERIE & being possible. Afterwards we went on foot at any post now occupied by 4th MB which has been kept well supplied by Lt. NICE. We also saw the new advt post of the 1st ABRFC + returned on improvement on the former.	
			The late Pm (initial)	
	29	9 a.m.	Adm: 3 odd + 1 off + 17 sick. Do Cas Clg Sta. 2 odd + 9 - Do Div. Res Sta 1 off + 3 - Do Bag.S. Amazing 35	

Army Form C. 2118.

WAR DIARY
or
INTELLIGENCE SUMMARY
(Erase heading not required.)

Instructions regarding War Diaries and Intelligence Summaries are contained in F.S. Regs., Part II. and the Staff Manual respectively. Title Pages will be prepared in manuscript.

Place	Date	Hour	Summary of Events and Information	Remarks and references to Appendices
ROLLEBEQUE FARM ARMENTIÈRES	Aug: 29	12 non	Rain began to fall & later descended in torrents. The night was cold.	# GGM
	30	9 a.m.	Adm: 2 add. + 14 S. - D.Cav. Cly.Sta. 100B - B.S.I.d. - D.Div: Rec.Sta:) D.Inf: 3. Amg: 34 Completed arrangements for filling place in res. Porte Byr: conj army trucks brigade the Artries remains in brid.	
	"	"	Admitted 2 wounded 48 S.I.d. D. Car. Cly. Sta. 2nd & 2.S. - D.Div. Rec.Sta. 10. D.Inf. 8. Amg. 32.	
	31	9.a.m.	Capt: STORROCK with C Section returned from ERQUINGHEM.	
		10.a.m.	Lt: MARPLOTE sent to bomb-school but his services were not required.	

27th/Division

121/6983

Confidential

War Diary
of
83rd Field Ambulance, R.A.M.C.

Vol IX
September, 1915.

WAR DIARY
or
INTELLIGENCE SUMMARY

(Erase heading not required.)

Army Form C. 2118

Instructions regarding War Diaries and Intelligence Summaries are contained in F.S. Regs., Part II. and the Staff Manual respectively. Title Pages will be prepared in manuscript.

Place	Date	Hour	Summary of Events and Information	Remarks and references to Appendices
HOULEPLOT FARM ARMENTIERES	Sept 1	5 a.m.	Lt SONNTAG returned from leave.	AAM
		9 a.m.	Adm: 1 wounded and 1 sick. To Cas. Clg. Stn: 4 sick. To Div: Rec'd Stn. 5 Trans: to 82nd Field Amb: 1 wdd & 4 sick. To Duty: 4. Remaining 26.	
		2 p.m.	Col: LIDDELL A.S.C. inspected Horse Transport.	
		2.30	Acceptance of M.O.L. Bell type cart was tried. Some exceptional points giving to highest specifications were noted.	
		3.20	Capt: A.E. DEVONALD proceeded to England on leave. Capt PIPER detailed after Bomb School and Lt CABOYD to take charge of medical arrangements & sanitation at Bge H.Q's.	
			Weather continued cold and there was a considerable amount of rain.	
	2	9 a.m.	Admitted 10 S. To Cas: Clg. Stn. 2. To Div: Rec'd Stn. 4. To Duty 2. Remg. 28.	
		10 a.m.	Lt CABOYD continued sanitation work at Bge HQs.	
		4 p.m.	Violent Cannonading heard on our left, continued some time.	
			A scheme of defence was read over our area, considered by the Senior officers of the unit.	
			Heavy rain fell during the day & night.	
			Admitted 11. To Cas: Clg Stn. 1. To Div: Rec'd Stn. Mec Stn. 8. Remg. 30	
	3	9 a.m.	Detailed Major GILLAM & Lt REGAN to inspect ESTAMINET Farm. Accommodation to be studied for HQs of the unit, but the offering of Transport section remains.	
		2 p.m.	Hallard with Capt PIPER Vet C.A. BOYD & experience in our important subject: ATNs C	
		3.30 p.m.	Office	

WAR DIARY
or
INTELLIGENCE SUMMARY
(Erase heading not required.)

Army Form C. 2118

Place	Date	Hour	Summary of Events and Information	Remarks and references to Appendices
BAILLEUL FARM MAEDENPEERS	Sept. 3		Usual routine. Weather continued overcast and cold.	W.J.G.K.
	4	9 a.m.	Admitted 9. To Cas. Cl. Sta: 4. To Base Rest Sta: 2. Remaining 34.	
		2 p.m.	Capt. PYPER & Capt. C.H. BOYD rode the right sector in order to make themselves (& transport) with mass medical situation. The result of the ride was to show that (i) he was that has been obtained are ample for the most part in the communication trenches. (ii) Dear though was to be used as B'd. Corps H.Q.S. (iii) the probability that in certain eventualities GAS POT would be untenable. (iv) the likelihood of establishing a dressing sta. in the neighbourhood of ERQUINGHEM for the R. at Coy on the Z of trenches.	
	5	9 a.m.	Adm. 1 ill. 3. To Cas. Cl. Sta: 10 ill. 8. To Base Rest Sta: 1. To Base & Remg 24.	
		5 p.m.	BARMS rode to Camp. Information that horses at ESTRADE refused to allow our transport to the billets at any of his farms. Decided to try to obtain other quarters. There was considerable improvement in the weather in the course of the day.	
	6	9 a.m.	Admitted 9. To Cas. Cl. Sta: 4. To Base Cl. Sta: 3. Remaining 26.	
		11 a.m.	Went with L. MARKLOVE to see properties billed for transport at 1 am close to ESTRADE. Quite possible. Subsequently saw B.A.D.M.S. who said that he might secure it if we did not be too fire - out 20th Br. Munitions Column.	
	7	3 p.m.	B.A.D.M.S. ride to the Camp.	
		9 a.m.	Adm. 12. To C.C.S.: 9. To Br. Rest Sta. 1. To B Sta 2. Remg: 26. Secured POLLOT: C.R.E. PIN Jam. for Transport and with Capt. STORROCK in the course of the day made arrangement with Major WILLAN for coming to ESTRADE. Weather continued bright & warm.	

WAR DIARY or INTELLIGENCE SUMMARY

Army Form C. 2118

Place	Date	Hour	Summary of Events and Information	Remarks and references to Appendices
MALLEBEQUE FARM	Sept 8	9 a.m.	Adv: Dr. Q - Do Cas: Cy: Sta: Q - Do Div: Mon-Sta: 3 - Do Bef: 3 - Army: 23	HGM
ARMENTIERES		10. a.m	Lt Col BRACKENRIDGE, on appointment as ADMS XII C Army Corps, relinquished two post and SADMS - XXVII & Divn.	
		2 p.m.	Lt Col Ormonde KEOGH proceeded to England on leave.	
		3 p.m.	Lt E.H. FENNESSY and Lt Col Rev. M. POWELL of 70th F. Amb (23rd Divn) were attached for instruction at platforms. The day was quiet. At night there was a considerable amount of rifle fire, some machine gun fire, very little gunfire.	
			Mr: P. COMEAU reported on return from leave.	
	9	4. a.m.	Adv: 10 N.Z.S. - Do Cas: Cy: Sta: 8 - Do Div: Rest-Sta: 2 - Do Bef: 3 - Army: 20.	
		9 a.m.	Day was again the ordinary.	
			Capt A.E. DEVONALD and Mr. J. KELLY reported on return from leave.	
	10	4 a.m.	Adv: 14 - Do Cas: Cy: Sta: 6 - Do Div: Rest-Sta: 2	
		9 a.m.	A Regimental Court Martial was convened by O.C. unit for trial of Capt S. WEEDON and JENNINGS - on the charge (i) absent from parade without leave. (ii) travelling by motor Amb.	
		10. a.m	together without permission. The Court sat till 1.10 p.m. proceeded at 2.30 p.m. at H.15 p.m. The two prisoners were found guilty on both counts in the case of Capt WEE- Don't with strong mitigating circumstances. In the case of Capt JENNINGS no extenuating circumstances. The Sentences are: Capt WEEDON, reduction to rank of 1st Capt. Capt JENNINGS, reduction to rank of Private. Being severely dispraised. Members of Court: Capt PIPER (President), Capt MORNEYER and Lieut FREITMAYER, A.S.C.	

WAR DIARY
or
INTELLIGENCE SUMMARY
(Erase heading not required.)

Army Form C. 2118

Place	Date	Hour	Summary of Events and Information	Remarks and references to Appendices
HOLLEBEQUE FARM ARMENTIERES	Sep 10		The day & night on our immediate front remained quiet. News was sent in from GHQ of an important Russian success in Galicia. Fine warm weather with cool breeze continued.	ADSSM
	11	9 a.m.	Admitted 10. To Cas. Cly: St: 7. To Fd Rest Sta H - To duty 3 - R sng: 21.	
		2 p.m	Lt FENNESSY Lt & Qr mr POWELL with NCOs & men left the camp returned their own and -	
		5 p.m	Lt A. FARQUHAR, 70 Lt 3.A., 23rd Division, arrived, attached for further Instruction. Major WARD with newly appointed RAMC, 2/Lt Division, rode the billets -	
			Adm: 10 occds, GQ wounded (Bomb-school) & 8 sick - To Cas. Cly: St: 12 To duty 2. Rmaing 25. Informed by RAMC of Intention of ADMS to attach 2 Sections by to Divl Cav. Sqn for - the Divisional purposes. Part to our line in front of F. No 93 accommodation being arranged that the neighbouring farm might be available as a billet. He was agreed to - later NCO from Transport & NCO i/c Water-cart were sent over to see in the matter of water. Received same time information of proposed re-arrangements of our Amb men. - The London Gazette II th inst: contained the following: Major H.G.G. Mackenzie M.D. to be temp'y: Lt. Col. (Sgn 11) Capt — to be Starred M.D. to be temp Major (Sgn 11)	
	12	9 a.m. 9:30 a.m		
		4.30pm	Detachments of Sqn & 3 Amb. arrived. Took up quarters & neighbouring farm. Day & night remained quiet. Informed in course of day of probable further removal of Division, with the 3 D Amb into the area of another Corps.	

WAR DIARY
or
INTELLIGENCE SUMMARY
(Erase heading not required.)

Army Form C. 2118

Place	Date	Hour	Summary of Events and Information	Remarks and references to Appendices
HOLLEBEKE FARM ARMENTIERES	Sept 13	6.30 a.m.	An enemy plane of the "Aviatik" type was attacked & too air almost immediately above the Camp by a British machine and appeared disabled. The pilot was able to steer on to and landed not far from STEENWERCK, Haggard that his first task was finished. In landing one of the airmen afford a machine gun fire to a Company of KRR which was passing – reinforcements would not returns the fire. The key opened a fire with rifles & killed the two airmen. The machine was to H/ard capture.	HGM
		9 a.m.	Adm: 1 off +8. 2o Cas. Cg. St: 8 20 Div. Rest Sta: 1 off. 2o Day 3 Remaining 32. ROMS H.Q. Capt visited Camp Reported the strong gratitude with manner in which the unit had performed its duties while attacked & th'd Capt. He expressed his satisfaction was	
		12 noon	orders Reorganize on Part II order mod out to the unit on parade. During the course of the day various threats were received. The unit was to march at 3 p.m. to 14 to an unknown destination understood to be about 11 miles distant. All equipment supplies to mobilization equipment was to be handed over to army and (67 & 2 Amb). The trappers were half packs Jackets Lug to day – the weather still remaining fine.	
		6 p.m.	Brig Sir Gen: SMITH GOC 8th Bde + visited Camp + arranged for motor amb bys Befor Brigade + field of stragglers. Capt PYPER detailed for this duty.	
14		6 a.m.	Weather cloudy but trip began. & fell & showers.	
		9 a.m.	Adm Ad 12. 2o Cas. Cg. St: 16. 20 Div. Nei St:) 20 day J Remaining 15. All the whom brought to Amb by aux. displ'd of before the horr of departure ROMS visited Camp + stated as to march close behind to Pot Byde until 4.30.3	
		10 a.m.	Orders were received	

1875 Wt. W593/826 1,000,000 4/15 J.B.C. & A. A.D.S.S./Forms/C.2118.

WAR DIARY
INTELLIGENCE SUMMARY

Army Form C. 2118

Place	Date	Hour	Summary of Events and Information	Remarks and references to Appendices
HOUPLINES FARM ARMENTIÈRES	Sep 14	2.45p	The Field Ambulance proceeded to STRAZEELE by MERRIS - MERVILLE = STEENWERCK = LE VERRIER = MERRIS - STRAZEELE. The usual halts were allowed. The men marched splendidly & while there was a great strain in the transport. At MERRIS Major STURROCK proceeded to STRAZEELE & LYNARXORE who had been sent on as billeting officer some hours before. Our billets were in a farm to S.E. of village - from each before we arrived. Two there was no difficulty, the transport being most sufficiently handled. Capt HYPER with 3 horse ambulance waggons followed the Both Brigade & dealt with casualties occurring en route. He reports that more men fell out than used to be expected - but a high proportion by these came from Sanitary Section & Bath detail - Viz. men who had not been selected as not fit to marching.	#G5th
STRAZEELE	15	9 a.m.	The reporter after a threatening morning remained fine. Proceeded to Brigade HQs & arranged that AMOS should be notified that all no. vehicle of King to be evacuated shortly as possible to ADCS A Eileen Cars. Again. Evacuation we would transfer to HAZEBROUCK or elsewhere - Standing Garrison proceed to HAZEBROUCK and enquire if there were any difficulty about sending by 2 Cas. Cly. Sta. there a few such cases. However, if the HAs were sent on in the course of the day. These arrangements were approved by AMSMS 2) of Division who made STRAZEELE later in the day.	
		6pm.	A good deal of stacking of waggons with a view to great mobility was carried out at KREITRHAYE & announced that he had agreed to the area and decided on the 18th forces.	

Army Form C. 2118

WAR DIARY
or
INTELLIGENCE SUMMARY
(Erase heading not required.)

Instructions regarding War Diaries and Intelligence Summaries are contained in F. S. Regs, Part II. and the Staff Manual respectively. Title Pages will be prepared in manuscript.

Place	Date	Hour	Summary of Events and Information	Remarks and references to Appendices
STRAZEELE	Sept 16	4.30am	Lt. v Donnell KEOGH started on return from leave.	AAQM
		9 a.m.	Motor-bicyclists came in during the day. Some were proceeded to HAZEBROUCK. In answer to a demand from Genl. WOC made the following recommendations in relation to the fights round YPRES April 22 = May 27 :-	
			Lt. C.A. BOYD — Military Cross. C.Q.M.S. WALKER (M.T. M.S.E.) Mention. Pte DOLTON	
		11 a.m	ADMS visits billet.	
		10.30pm	Sgt Bk. 00 received states that up to 3 Amb's arrived station at THIENNES, the four probably about 6 a.m on 18th.	
	—17	9.30 am	Amb's arrived and started our return agreeably of morning Amb. by jog approached at Motor Ambulance station by eight Hars. Proceed. Sgt Major STURROCK met CABOYO to collect orders. On return found Jr & Majeret road Elead. 0 on station piece of work for which credit & Sgt Ball (unite) to return KEOGH.	
THIENNES	—18	12.45	The Ford Amb. detached to THIENNES STATION not arrived, pts arrived at 6 6 a.m. Jnitrout was could suffer in transit. The partie but the room.	
		5 am	The dragoons were also lodged on the Ind. well with refreshments. Breakfast was for the men before starting.	
		8.20 am	Dr. nung guns & new guns. A long Sgt (Horn) went at ABBEVILLE at 3.pm. about an carrier w picket lice Lorne. Found saund. The jorny was 85 Ret.	

1875 Wt. W593/826 1,000,000 4/15 J.B.C. & A. A.D.S.S./Forms/C. 2118.

Army Form C. 2118

Instructions regarding War Diaries and Intelligence Summaries are contained in F. S. Regs., Part II. and the Staff Manual respectively. Title Pages will be prepared in manuscript.

WAR DIARY
or
INTELLIGENCE SUMMARY
(Erase heading not required.)

Place	Date	Hour	Summary of Events and Information	Remarks and references to Appendices
GUILLANCOURT COURT	Sept 18	7.30 p.m	No Stop was made at AMIENS. The two half armed detachments (GUILLANCOURT) & hour rehearse between one again for orders. Orders the stor of ASMs and Insp COLLEN (ADS 2/A Div) the 3 Amb. proceeded as 9 p.m. to MORCOURT where Capt DEDONALD had erected a suitable field for a night bivouac.	#AAM
MORCOURT	19	8.30 a.m	O.C. 9 Amb with Major STURROCK & Pr. C. A. BOYD rode under direction of POR KHARRENTMAYER advanced dressing station — CAPPY, ad posts & dressing stations at CAPPY and ??? ? Station adjacent. CAPPY. He a preliminary Major STURROCK would take at 4 p.m. but 2 officers & C.A.BOYD & orderlies and a small detachment. The establishment of the rest of the staff & decay of was a Risk a.a.c. difficult matter. He had of accommodation made any setback unnecessary difficult. Arrangements from that decided to have the staff & FROISSY with the 3rd followers among an arrangement which would perhaps hold for 3 or 4 days until some other place could be found.	
	20.	6 a.m	Right and front together the entire convoy was continuous. It was BOYD and the small detachment to FROISSY and Staff to MORCOURT. He was unsure at 9 a.m. Some sick are picked up at Hidden Brigade Hospital & sent to hospital at by 3 Amb. There now no casualties. Saw officer courts of No. 10 M.A.C. Arrange for the one & may take car	

1875 Wt. W593/826 1,000,000 4/15 J.B.C. & A. A.D.S.S./Forms/C. 2118.

WAR DIARY
or
INTELLIGENCE SUMMARY

(Erase heading not required.)

Army Form C. 2118

Place	Date	Hour	Summary of Events and Information	Remarks and references to Appendices
ERCUISY	Sep 20		At 7 & 3 Bdy collected numbers of the evacuated cases and the purpose according. Subsequent arranged with Major STURROCK to send down two motor-lorries. Also asked Byde Hdqts to advise RMOs of Brigade.	Again
		9am	Accompanied ADMS to see Chief Medical Officer of probable occupation by Bns FAMB. Secured first vacated by French at CHUIGNOLLES and another place at CHUIGNOLLES. Lt JSN BOYD with small detachment went to former place to hold until RAMC arrived. Our ambulance the only place that seems probable was not too far back, was in the identical below but ADMS promises to try to obtain suitable quarters by arrangement with 5th Division.	
			Div Hosp changed into a today. Informed ADMS that the village of LA NEUVILLE (the cabine above-mentioned) was now in our area rather we and the regimental aid. Preceded with Col DESMOND, had a conf. of the Bde unit who has no bearing arrangement. The points but one have now been filled at a pressing St LAps of a Amb. Be took the one ………. many Germans have settled for the transport.	
			After first came to the Durre of the day was the genuine of DESMOND Rest Sta a matter of urgent importance. The genuine of Divin avarage is the worst.	

WAR DIARY
or
INTELLIGENCE SUMMARY

Army Form C. 2118

Place	Date	Hour	Summary of Events and Information	Remarks and references to Appendices
FROISSY	Sep 21	12 noon	[illegible handwritten entry regarding orders and arrangements for convoy and billets over the next few days. Morning.]	Appx
		2pm	The D.A.D.S. moved to LA NEUVILLE. Took up the inspection — In many ways commodious and suitable. The are not many rooms to arrange & the best advantage. Good accommodation for men and detailed men houses secured at once. Rooms of pitch — that the whole place seems to be overrun with rats.	
		4pm	A.D.M.S. + D.A.D.M.S. rode into billet. He met C.O. 1 Section and C Section near by & CAPPY. Major SURROCK had two Sections of C Section but C Section instead for dirty armed fairs, the one others. He took off chiens up the billet proceeded. Points could be made comfortable from the beginning. Casualties were still light. So the few huts got with the erection of the timber sheds at about 2 about 25 though if offices would below the parapet throughout this seems these so would casualties.	
LA NEUVILLE in BRAY	22	12 noon	Adm: 2 wounded 3 sick. D.CCSA: 20 + 35. D.A.D.S. 1 Army O.	
		3pm	Instructed ADMS to find site for Divisional Baths	
		6pm	AN SMSM asepthaea was his ambulance given of a Bath place arrangement followed in the Major of MABEAT	
	23	10 a.m.	The ambulance declared more than I used to have been effect for caution and this has been going on round to medical men in front of an advance to release next. At the same gap it was arranged that a round from the B.B.C Hqs on subject of offices tent not fixing to the front of the railway to be called together about 10 to letting the village of and be on medical should tough altar of horse — more permanent arrangement could if made to Brigade Hqrs.	

Army Form C. 2118

WAR DIARY
or
INTELLIGENCE SUMMARY
(Erase heading not required.)

Instructions regarding War Diaries and Intelligence Summaries are contained in F.S. Regs., Part II and the Staff Manual respectively. Title Pages will be prepared in manuscript.

Place	Date	Hour	Summary of Events and Information	Remarks and references to Appendices
LA NEUVILLE les BRAY	Sep 23	12 noon	Adm ITO 1 off + 2 other + 10 sick. To Cas: Cly: Sta: 2 OR 3 w/sick. 1 officer died of wounds. Remaining O.	WGM
			The afternoon passed off quietly. Our guns were active. A thunderstorm came up towards evening rain continued throughout the night rain for fill hours. The weather however continued warm.	
	24	10 a.m.	Reports to ADMS that hardly any building in Bernafay were found to be suitable for billets. Recommended that ruined factory at FROISSY might be put in order and troops & officers billeted there accommodated in huts or the like erected for that purpose. ADMS of Lake Div intimated that Divisional Res: Stn (actually not at the present site in front that 50 cases. All 3 F.Ambulances must retain their mobility. Division was evacuating a heavy wastage from sickness.	
		12 noon	Adm 2 other + 18 sick. To Cas: Cly: Sta: 2 OR 3 w/sick. To Cas: Cly: Sta: 2 OR 3 w/sick. To dut other 3: 0.	
		3 p.m.	Visited Adv: Dress Stn n/infected Sanitation of billets of H.Q.FAC + 4/R.B. at Carnoy. The work is all in hand. The chief difficulty is the provision of empty tins for latrines. The French inhabitants are usually told (constatée).	
			Our guns were again active in the afternoon but provoked practically no reply from the enemy. Battery together lay quiet and worked in accordance with orders. An occasional false alarm was reported but contradicted soon.	
	25	8 a.m.	Work done since May 27:	
			Major W. D. STURROCK, Lt R.A.M.C. J. KEOGH, A: C.S.M. SEARLE N.T., ASC H.T., S-S MILDRED HALL W.G., S-S BOSLEY N.F., L: Cap: CALLAWAY S.A., Pte HOPKINS M, ASC M.T.	

Army Form C. 2118

WAR DIARY or INTELLIGENCE SUMMARY

(Erase heading not required.)

Instructions regarding War Diaries and Intelligence Summaries are contained in F.S. Regs., Part II. and the Staff Manual respectively. Title Pages will be prepared in manuscript.

Place	Date	Hour	Summary of Events and Information	Remarks and references to Appendices
LA NEUVILLE 1. BRAY	Sep 25	12 mn	Adm: Ladders - 1 off + y.s. All Am KCSR. 30 bags of sand. Inspected billets at FRAISSEY. A good deal remains to be done before sanitation of the area can be called satisfactory.	AGGM
		3 pm	Official news from Trois-Saints succeeds near LENS including capture of guns, also of a French attack in CHAMPAGNE.	
		6 pm	Sitting with Major Grice and G. Smit Lt. R.F. SONNTAG & 82nd Inf.B. Capt. A GRIFFITH is temporary in/c. the Batn. He present system of only one officer to unit at the front is an appalling hotchpotch any with an intention (if they are T.D.) that a T.C. officer is to be attached in order to effect make him fit for them. O.C. 2nd Inf.B. with A. Kitmayer noted L. Schr near Hopsy M.O. also in charge Signoteur as to where no hope from our approach to the minelos they attach to wire Day In the start of war fine. He walks to Lobricay. The difficulties in every good and in any gone.	
26		10 am	Official report spoke of a check to the Such advance, the N and S Captains 3 the North of Y. 3000 prisoners in CHAMPAGNE. No firm news from Los de Bethonaire there was much talk of an advance there. Mahus noted killed a Afficer Cohen	
		3 pm	After M. Inf.B. Coggina send to Inoble there to day Feb will was possible. O.C.	

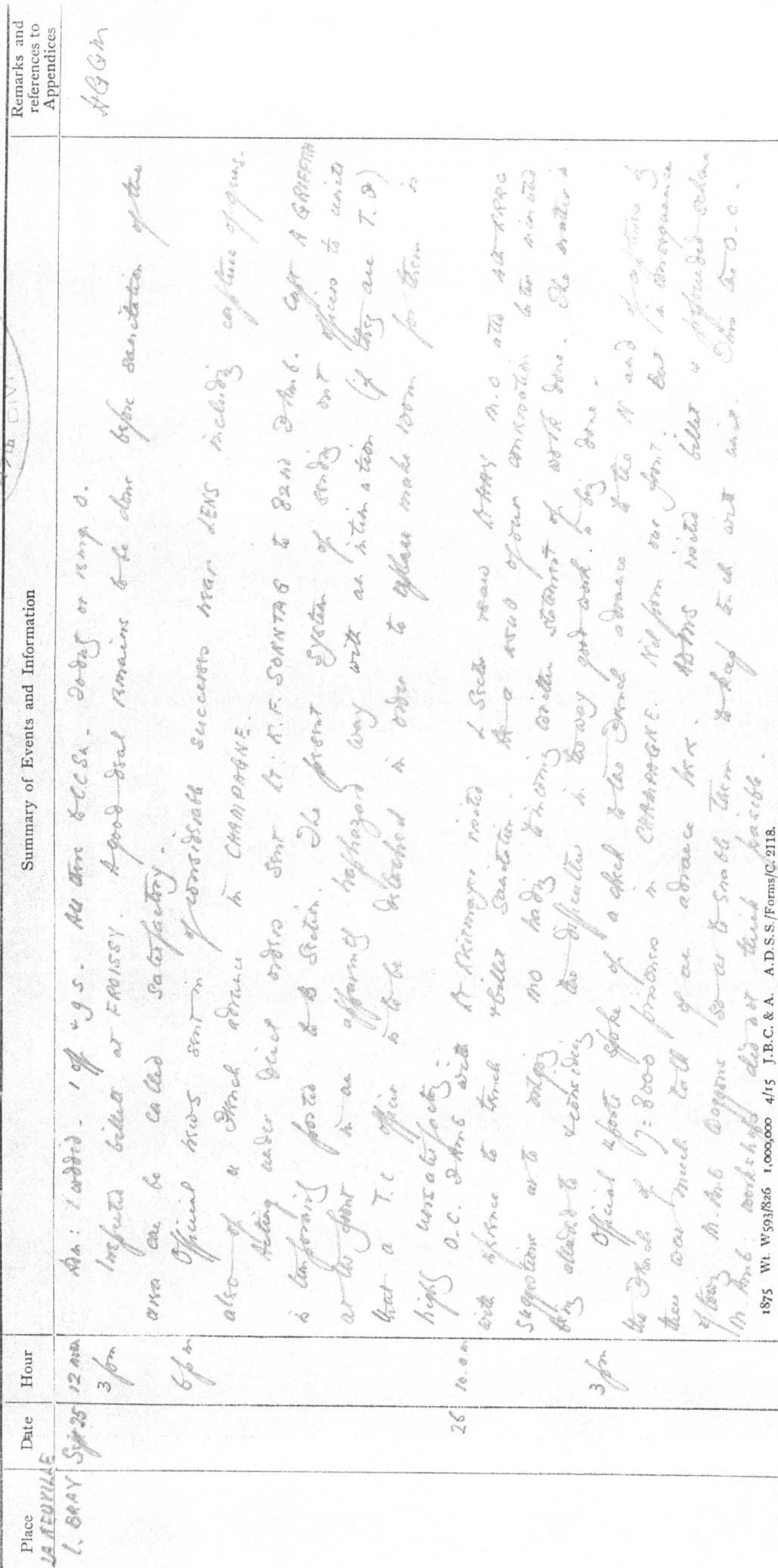

WAR DIARY
or
INTELLIGENCE SUMMARY

(Erase heading not required.)

Army Form C. 2118

Instructions regarding War Diaries and Intelligence Summaries are contained in F.S. Regs., Part II. and the Staff Manual respectively. Title Pages will be prepared in manuscript.

27th [stamp]

Place	Date	Hour	Summary of Events and Information	Remarks and references to Appendices
MEOVILLE to BRAY	Sep 28		W.MOs came & gave orders for days work.	HGGM
	27/	7.30am	The flowing officers were attached for instructional purposes from 80% Field Ambulance: Capt. B. JOHNSON (O.C.), Lt. C.L. WIGAN, Lt. A.A. WILSON, Lt. & Q.M.F.J. PAYNE. with 4 NCOs & 19 men.	
		11 am	HQMs ordered JA to take charge of a hospital barge which was said to have accommodation for 40 patients. This and the moored near CAPPY and to be stores of Capt. GRIFFITH under direction of Major STURROCK. The official communiqué from 2nd British Sources confirmed news of recent successes. On the battle front 46 guns were captured up to date, a large number of machine guns & a great quantity of material with 30,000 wounded prisoners.	
		1 pm	Officer i/c of 80th F.Amb. rooted as Res.G. Ly/11th was the scene. The following officers were from 29th Field Ambulance were attached for instructional purposes: Capt. P.S. TOMLINSON, Lt. F.G. FRASER, Lt. D.J. STOKES, Lt. R.J. HEARN, Lt. P.C. DAVIE, Lt. & Qmr. A. JACKSON with 4 NCOs & 19 men. Usual instruction was given in practical side of F. Amb. work.	
	28	8 am	Adm: 1 off. + 4 ord. wh. All sick. To C.C.S. this day. Today returning O.C. & Official news reach Hqrs today. Relates to the obliteration of fame. No orders for forecast of advance on our front. Sent were received. Funeral Divisional office on subject of Bouflers came in.	

Army Form C. 2118

WAR DIARY
or
INTELLIGENCE SUMMARY
(Erase heading not required.)

Place	Date	Hour	Summary of Events and Information	Remarks and references to Appendices
LA NEUVILLE & BRAY	Sept 28	7 pm	Other ranks of 29th D Amb: visited aid posts on both sides of L sector. The circular had by this time completely broken, and the usual midnight of deep mud & slime may be expected as normal accompaniment of the next fortnight. This is worse, if Somme worse, on the "Shogshire" side than the "BRAY" side. The tractors had all failed. A Certain amount of vigorous gunfire was heard from the right. No efforts to our men from our own subs guns.	HQ GM 
	29	10 a.m	Hospital Barge arrived near FROISSY - later made FROISSY. Water was complete arrangements to know. It was the near FROISSY but the supplies from our own car from the Amb cars the ship except there to which immediate operation was indicated. O.C. Barge & tarry beds NAMES. O.C. Barge & tarry beds NAMES. O.C. Division + BAMS Arranged with O.S.C. of the 58 & DAMb be the terms of pay MAMS. O.C. Division + BAMS Shown all came up VA Stn 3. to collecting work and After some morning instruction Rather more than one another that one the better general to include the never report that one the general has in clothes fire was heard. There was R/ker gunfire, thus considerable amount of rifle machine gun	
	30	5 a.m	Usual situation was given to officers of 29th & 88th D A. who had been round the aid posts the previous night.	

WAR DIARY or INTELLIGENCE SUMMARY

Army Form C. 2118

Place	Date	Hour	Summary of Events and Information	Remarks and references to Appendices
LA NEUVILLE 1. MAY	Sep 30	4.30	Sent down 3 barges had all 3 barges moored in a position & what is is almost impossible & much time by a motor amb: wagon many & sowing natives of wounded. Tryed took on 2 barges but of pants the position should be changed to other side of canal. Unor a horse amb: wagon must to to ard). The oth Divn have now horse [bgn?] have their two barges — The tiger bar available for heavy retentions rifle machine gun he your gun fire from our guns. The enemy did not try to take the trepments some high explosive shells of high caliber came over. The wound casualties of the shell meets whether & of admixation or in the front sector have been few. Nor has the sick incidence been high. Our a ... effective personnel (which need not me: be divisional) remains as obtains many more proportify to be a shortage if the case of the Star has an increased clerical staff and "elsewhere" a till sorter - to be not set as well as down the line.	A.D.M.S.

1875 Wt. W593/826 1,000,000 4/15 J.B.C. & A. A.D.S.S./Forms/C. 2118.

27th Division
and

/21/
7570

Confidential

War Diary

of

83rd Field Ambulance, R.A.M.C. T.F.

October, 1915.

Vol X

Army Form C. 2118

WAR DIARY
or
INTELLIGENCE SUMMARY
(Erase heading not required.)

Instructions regarding War Diaries and Intelligence Summaries are contained in F. S. Regs., Part II. and the Staff Manual respectively. Title Pages will be prepared in manuscript.

Place	Date	Hour	Summary of Events and Information	Remarks and references to Appendices
LA NEUVILLE				AOGM
1. BRAY	Oct.1	10 a.m.	Received intimation that hospital barge no. 140 was to be moored on this side of canal near FROISSY bridge as possible & that a road capable of bearing motor vehicles would be constructed & used.	
		6 pm	Saw non-coms. officers of No. 140 J Amb. arrived for instruction. Arranged with O.C. Pg to J Amb. for instruction, & am sending the usual details the following morng. Arranged with O.C. 80 to J Amb. to send orderlies & motor as he thought desirable up to J officers & other ranks. Heavy cannonade some night. We were told to our North being tonight.	
	2	11 am	ADMS called regarding various matters in respect of Batts & Barge no. It is to be regarded as a ward of the Ostrog. & is — patients something not to be booked on N.B. books as transferred.	
		12 noon	Admitted 3 wounded & 9 sick. B. Lee. Cpl. Sgt. Barrack & 6 sick. ORS.-Rmg.-23. Railway car for, but fastened by old & a large wooden Some horrarger. The first that came & convoy of Sgt. ORs are transferred to base.	
	3	9 am	First a detailed intimation of billets and transport lines Billets are in a satisfactory	
		11 a.m.	Saying set RMO. on subject of finds that orderlies officers believed to at least be left to be sent of night to the ORs.	
		12 noon	Admitted 8 sick. Sa Lee. Cpl. St. Said. Remarking 3 wounded residents. News came in Eng. Say that supposed not an attempt at a force advance now	
LENS			So far unsuccessful	

WAR DIARY
INTELLIGENCE SUMMARY

Army Form C. 2118

Place	Date	Hour	Summary of Events and Information	Remarks and references to Appendices
La NEUVILLE	Oct 3		Evening & night remained quiet.	A,G & h
w BRAY	4	10 a.m.	BMS of Army announced to-night that nightly DAMS; but did not arrive. ADMS of VIII Corps & D.D.M.S 2 Corps & Major Marrowe motored calls carried through	
		12 noon	A good deal of work was done & made up trench feet preparation. Capt MARLOWE was detailed for the work. Anti-foot vaccine was issued with 1 in 20 mustard. Some of the night last - the 4 Brigade Gazette issued 100 next day. Horses suffered hurt sufficient 100 lbs - the following found 100 next day. London Gazette and announcement of promotion of Lt. J.C. MARLOWE to Capt. 1st dated 20th May.	
	5		News received that British forces N of LENS were holding their own against H.Q.s Adm: 2 add VII sick - To CCS 2 add & 8 sick - To Bgd Rest Stn 3 - Rmg - 23 O.C's i/c Bearers called. Head that No. 140 add Jord. remain here and the other 2 units (3rd Dev.) to be moved higher up the canal.	
		7 p.m.	Orders to take control on Col of Brigade Baths at CAPPY. Sergt LOCKHURST & pts GOSDEN detailed to superintend arrangements.	
			A large supply of trench feet preparation sent up to CAPPY for distribution to aid post ADMS and ADMS of 26th Division provided billet Adm in transf: 3 wounded & 2 sick - To Cas. Cly Stn 3 wounded & 13 sick. To Div. Rest Stn 11. Remaining 26.	
		12 noon	Afternoon & night were exceptionally quiet.	

WAR DIARY or INTELLIGENCE SUMMARY

Army Form C. 2118

Place	Date	Hour	Summary of Events and Information	Remarks and references to Appendices
LA NEUVILLE (a) BRAY	Oct 7	11.30 a.m.	DMS 3rd Army Inspected Amb. Transport lines -	AGM
		12 noon	Adm. 5 wounded 1 officer & 10 sick - Do Cas: Clg. Sta: 1 wounded 1 off: 472 sick. Do Div. Rest Sta: = 2. Do Div S. 13 - Remaining 19 -	
	8	9 a.m.	Too bad a morning set about the arrangt of featureG began to try for items and to get new again bricks or tiles - Roof of shed spoke of difficult to obtain - Floors will again Proceeded to CAPPY to make various arrangemt re Baths - Do seem to be able to manage.	
		3.00	Returned via Bray from wit to Soyre stores -	
	9	12 noon	Adm. 11 sick. Do Cas. Cg. Sta: 1 Do Div. Rest Sta: 10. Army: 19. Morris paper contained big startling news from Balkans. A complete understanding of Central Powers with Bulgaria (said to exist) & no apparent to Servia relied looks for feer Greece. News from Champagne of a further French success with Capture of 1000 prisoners. Wrd in Barns anything satisfactory.	
	10	12 noon	Admitted 1 off 16 sick - Do Cas. Clg Sta: 1 off 8. Do Div: Rest Sta: 10 Army: 21. Proceeded to CAPPY & returned at some arrangemt of after Brigade sent in no return.	
		4 p.m.	DDMS Attd Surg 9 a.m. 6: with special reference to Expansion - Brilli Sophie h.q. I RACCI Transport lines -	
		3.30	Adm. 1 off. 14 mn. sick. Do Cas. Clg. Sta: 1 & 5. Do Div: Rest Sta: 9. Army: 9. Remaining 21 Pym made with Reps. to Farms for Expansion. In absence of bricks, timber are	
		12 noon	Chalk floors with rubble.	
	12	12 noon	Adm: 3 off 10 sick. Do Cas: Clg St. 3 off 13 sick - Do Div: Rest Sta: 6. Army 22. Asked Capt. E.W. Dearden deal with A.E. BEA. The first for many on the	
		10 p.m.	Not reported. Lac d. decv. mostent game -	
		8 a.m.	Major W.D. STURROCK proceeded to England on leave.	

Army Form C. 2118

WAR DIARY
or
INTELLIGENCE SUMMARY
(Erase heading not required.)

Instructions regarding War Diaries and Intelligence Summaries are contained in F. S. Regs., Part II. and the Staff Manual respectively. Title Pages will be prepared in manuscript.

Place	Date	Hour	Summary of Events and Information	Remarks and references to Appendices
C. BRAY	Oc.12	12 noon	Adm: 1 Off. & 1 W&D - 19 sick - 20 ECSS. 1 Off. N W&D - 7 sick - 20 Div. Mot. Sta: 8. 20 Inf. 8. Army.	ADGMS
LA NEUVILLE			18. Number of patients sick & sick high -	
			Heavy gunfire was heard to the N during the night -	
	13	12 noon	Adm. 1 off & 19 sick. 20 ECSS. 2 W&D & 2 sick. 20 Div. Mot Sta. 1. 20 Inf. 1. Army 1.	
			Motor cars in the afternoon of stretcher & bearers made 3 British troops	
		9 pm	Some shells began falling over BRAY. 5 were heard. These fell directly over 1 Sept. 8R.D. All	
			appeared to fall harmless near the BRAY - ALBERT road -	
	14	10 am	Sour officers & 14 ghts ranks came from 23 Div. IF&D for instructions & proceeded to CAPPY.	
		12 noon	Adm. 1 W&D Gr Sta.	
	15	9 am	Adm. 11 S. 20 Cav Cy Sta 2 20 Mot. Sta. C. Army 20.	
			Wishes the area find at Bry during day or night -	
			Proceed to CAPPY with ADMS (Photo medical board) in to officer of 30 to offer - Cas-	
			didate to Commodore in regular army.	
			Arrangements for removals on relief are now complete.	
			Weather had become very cold -	
		12 noon	Adm. 2 W&D & 16 sick 20 CCSA 2 W&D & 3 S. 20 Div. Mot. Sta. 9. 20 Inf. 2. Army. 21	
	16	10 am	Infi. casualties occurred day last 48 hours & appearing but greater and Made	
			Cht. BOYLOPP & make final arrangements for Non. Capt. LUCKHURST.	
			ASM (1 W&D) & 6 sick. 20 ECSH. 1 W&D. 20 Div. Mot. Sta. 7. Army 23	
		12 noon	almost complete quietude on my front for men at of Bry. Marlboro' Guns Army 7	
	17	11 am	Orders came to attach an officer & M.O. for remainder of war.	
			Brasils Cyr J.S.R. BOYD.	

Army Form C. 2118

WAR DIARY
or
INTELLIGENCE SUMMARY
(Erase heading not required.)

Instructions regarding War Diaries and Intelligence Summaries are contained in F.S. Regs., Part II. and the Staff Manual respectively. Title Pages will be prepared in manuscript.

Place	Date	Hour	Summary of Events and Information	Remarks and references to Appendices
La NEUVILLE				AA&QM
& BRAY	Oct 17	11 a.m.	Ordered to keep breast of Germans in order that after Bns of 88th Bgde practised Out return PROVART. two lorries motor conveyance from MARFUSEE. C Section meets AT Br St. at CAPPY. Took our horses AT MARFUSEE. 82nd Jam 6 coming in to CAPPY. Approached at CABOYO towards in charge of C Section.	
	18	12 noon	A&m 1 off and 412 Sed to Les Alyses 1 off ord. Jo Basai j. Jo Sg 2. Rmg 24.	
		6 a.m.	Weather became suddenly much colder, supporting East Wind.	
		12 noon	A8m 18 Sed. Jo CCSn. 1. Jo Sg 6. Remain 33.	
		2 p.m.	Moto billets at PROVART. Need for entering between outposts on coming units 10 BS evident.	
	19	12 noon	Heard that of our rifle machine gun fire was heard during 3 night. Remain 2. Jo Rly Aust Sn. 1. Jo Sg 2. Remain 30.	
		2.30 pm	Battn CAPPY begs in FROISSY.	
	20	10 a.m.	Vague reports at outset of Genl fighting between Bulgarians & Turks. No official confirmation. There was Distour to CHOIGNES to arrange for visiting the R sector - also Cage with ASAC.	
		12 noon	A&m little 4. Jo Bn. Arrivals 2. Gas 1. Remain 31.	
		4 pm	Rumour of no definite move to mi- area was intended. Various pressure that on our front.	
	21	9 a.m.	Taken in consequence. Major STEWART reported on return from leave. of the above general measure taken to dispose of personal material. Packing was delicately carried out and for ability for instanf, 1 off ow MSied. CCS 172. JP Sn. 3. Jo Sg 17. Remain 30.	
		12 noon	Information received that offensive suggested a move on 24th to some place near Amiens.	

1875 Wt. W.593/826 1,000,000 4/15 J.B.C.& A. A.D.S.S./Forms/C. 2118.

WAR DIARY or INTELLIGENCE SUMMARY

Army Form C. 2118

Place	Date	Hour	Summary of Events and Information	Remarks and references to Appendices
BRAY / LA NEUVILLE	Oct 22	9 a.m.	Proceeded to BRAY & ETINGHEM to arrange for transfer of sick & stores to St Riquier Magnetic adv. came to us to go to Etaples with O.R.s. 26 & 3rd D.Amb. was it. The latter was also to take over Dr. Bassey Sec. at CAPPY. Issued orders accordingly. Major SHURROCK to stand fast to look after stores. Stand fast preparation of body section for John Burton at MORCOURT. Arrang'd with Q to keep base workshop & settle question of evacuation. None admitted.	W.G.M.
	23	12 noon	To C.C.S. 4. To Base 2. Remaining 28.	
		3 pm	Capt PYPER reported for duty at CAPPY & relief of 2nd D.Amb.	
		12 noon	Adm: 4. To C.C.S.a 3. Remaining 9.	
	24		Various orders received. Busy day in reference to men. O.R.s are to leave last morning. Those to march & those to ride. Those to have some tomorrow to the stores this are that it will be possible to hand over to Dr. Sec. to French troops.	
		3 pm	The barge (140) left PROISSY refs to A.D.M.S. 3rd Div. at CHIPILLY.	
			Pte A.G. FLETCHER C.F. (C.E.) reported as attached to 3rd A/Sgt. Byles, railway. subsequently transferred to go A.S.R. by A.S.C.	
		12 noon	Adm: 9. To C.C.S.a Cy St. 3. To Ba. R01 02: 3.	
	25	12 nn	Lt.Col. MACKENZIE left on leave.	W.D.S.
	26	7.30 pm	Adm. 3. To C.C.S. 5. Remaining 15. F/ Amb. left LA NEUVILLE at 7.30. a.m.; arrived MORCOURT 9.30 a.m. Capt.	
MORCOURT				

WAR DIARY or INTELLIGENCE SUMMARY

Army Form C. 2118

Place	Date	Hour	Summary of Events and Information	Remarks and references to Appendices
MORCOURT	26th	7.30 a.m. (contd)	Pyr't party from Adv. Arming (Estr) joined up at FROISSY bridge, & afterwards went to ABANCOURT thus completing "C" section. Horsed ambulance followed infantry of 80 st. Brigade to ABANCOURT at 4 a.m. & 7 a.m., & to MORCOURT at 5 a.m. Capt DEVONALD delivered a Frenchwoman of a male child at MORCOURT at 5.15 p.m.	W.D.
BOVES	27th	7.30 p.m.	F'd Amb. left MORCOURT at 8.30 a.m., & arrived at BOVES at 2.45 p.m. Picking up "C" section on the way at ABANCOURT. Fine weather. Capt GRIFFITH was sent on in advance and obtained an entertainment room for a hospital; there was put under charge of Lt. C.A. BOYD, & heats from C section. Remainder of F'd Amb. under canvas.	
FLUY	28th	7.30 p.m.	F'd Amb. left BOVES at 9.45 a.m., & marched FLUY at 3 p.m.; had marched 4 miles of the route very bad in parts. Billetting, cookery & hospital party sent on with all motors, with orders to empty cars & return them at once to Lt. C.A. BOYD at BOVES. Brigade H.Q. issued orders to R.M.Os. to send all unfit men to BOVES hospital before starting march. The cars made 3 journeys from BOVES to FLUY & back & cleared 91 patients, with Lt BOYD's party & their equipment by 5.15 p.m. Some of them patients were returned to their unit after arrival, but some 70 were kept.	

Army Form C. 2118

WAR DIARY
or
INTELLIGENCE SUMMARY
(Erase heading not required.)

Instructions regarding War Diaries and Intelligence Summaries are contained in F.S. Regs., Part II. and the Staff Manual respectively. Title Pages will be prepared in manuscript.

Place	Date	Hour	Summary of Events and Information	Remarks and references to Appendices
FLUY.	29.10	6 p.m.	Return from noon on 26th to noon on 29th. Adm. 11. To 2 RC. 8. To C.C.S. 3. Remaining 6. Capt HARKLOVE detached for temporary duty with 4th KRRc.	Wet
"	30.	6 A.m.	Adm. Lt C.H. BOYD detached for temporary duty as D.A.D.M.S.	
"	31	6 p.m.	Adm. A.D.M.S. inspected "unfits" to 80th Inf. Brigade at 10.30 a.m. at H.Q. of the field ambulance.	
"	Nov 1.	6 p.m.	Adm. A.D.M.S. again inspected unfits of 80th Brigade at 11.30 a.m. Capt J.S.K. BOYD returned from duty with 2nd KOSLI & proceeded to England on leave.	
"	2.	12 noon	Lt Col A.G.G. MACKENZIE returned from leave. Adm. 20. T. C.C.S. 17. Remaining. 9.	

Confidential

War Diary
of
83rd Field Ambulance,
R.A.M.C. T.F.

November 1915

Vol XI

WAR DIARY
or
INTELLIGENCE SUMMARY

Army Form C. 2118

Place	Date	Hour	Summary of Events and Information	Remarks and references to Appendices
FLUJ	Nov. 1	11.30 am	ADMS again inspected "unit" of 80th Brigade. Capt J.S.R. BOYD returned from duty with 2nd A.F.A. and proceeded to England on leave.	ADSM
	2	9 am	Lt-Col A.G. MACKENZIE returned from leave.	
		12 noon	Adm. 20 – Do – C.Cl. St. 17 – Remaining 9.	
	3	9 am	Attended a conference of D.C. D.MS and ADMS' office. The question of substance far exceeded manner of structure was discussed – substance was certainly then. The question of transport which has not been settled may also be substituted of numbers was also discussed, but no definite conclusion was reached.	
		12 noon	Adm: 1 officer + 13 – Do-tar Cly 82 – off + 8 – Remaining X, X: 7 Proceed off to BETELLEES B. Midhurst ADMS (illegible) (illegible) made before to went in own.	
	4	1.30 pm	that a Genl Inspector of Billets	
			Remaining 7. D Col A.S. C.I. D Col F 6. Remaining 9.	
	5	9 am	Orders came to the effect that light draught horses were to be substituted for heavy draught, and that 4 in place of 6 were to go to each wagon. Also that 3 lumbers of agent were to be given up. The transport problem still remains acute.	
		12 noon	Adm: 11. Do-tar Cly: sec 11. Do-BuS 3. Remaining 8. One Car became a.s.o. Not Remaining well for November. BADMS visited hospital & said some "cases" of "cases".	
	6	11 am	Adm – 23 . Do-Bar Cly St. 11. to-B of 6. Remaining 16 .	
		12 noon	T.O. Morto Ludinoff of the Indies Motor Bund.	
			Car St. Lesirhant (Colonial Dispat Accord. Own Car & officer bar am Abc 20 in the afford bus illustrations stays member of additional Abc problems).	

WAR DIARY
or
INTELLIGENCE SUMMARY
(Erase heading not required.)

Army Form C. 2118

Place: FLOY

Date	Hour	Summary of Events and Information	Remarks and references to Appendices
Nov: 7	10 a.m.	Men rec'd attended Brigade service at REVELLES conducted by the Bishop of Khartoum	AGGM
	12 noon	Adm: Mil: 1.- To Cas: Cly Stn. 10.- To Infy 1.- Remains 12.-	
8	10.30	In the ordinary routine & transport were rec'd in the course of the day. An inspection of mules rang around part of it. The sun also seen (to be shining) guns and general transport.	
	12 noon	Adm: 19.- To Cas: Cly Stn. 5.- To Infy 1.- Remg: 15	
9	11 a.m.	Capt J.C. PYPER Evacuated Sick to St Michael Cas: Cly Stn ste AMIENS with Infy to Pyrexia	
	12 noon	Adm: 7. To Cas: Cly Stn 8. To Infy 5. Remg: 9.	
10		In the course of the day water or ground indeed hold war by half with some rain. The became one slough in the war line or trenches day: Major W.D. STURROCK, Capt: MARPLOVE, R! CLABOYD	
11	12 noon	Capt A.H.BREWER proceeded to England on short leave.	
	5 a.m.	Adm: 1 off 48.- To Cas: Cly Stn 1 off 48.- To Infy 2.- Remaining 7.-	
	11 a.m.	Capt A.E.DEVONALD proceeded to England on short leave.	
	12 noon	HMS visited the DA.M.S. with Spec: Men (M6,16 x) unfit for the trenches Adm: 3.- To Cas: Cly Stn. 3.- Remaining.	
	8 p.m.	Dark war sent to the officer of Station Minors to sentries guarding 40 additional ASC Piemont men. So to meet part this own by motor first quifts. Some	
12	9 a.m.	are without rifles. Rec'd orders to send for 1 riding horse 12 a/weapons for 1 amb: wagon, bits to complete	
	12 noon	our equipment. Adm: Mil. 11.- To Cas: Cly Stn 6.- To Infy 1.- Remain 11.-	

Army Form C. 2118

WAR DIARY
or
INTELLIGENCE SUMMARY
(Erase heading not required.)

Instructions regarding War Diaries and Intelligence Summaries are contained in F.S. Regs., Part II. and the Staff Manual respectively. Title Pages will be prepared in manuscript.

Place	Date	Hour	Summary of Events and Information	Remarks and references to Appendices
FLUY	Nov. 12	3 pm	Went out to ADMS's office to enqe as various infor. and points. No definite information as to date of move had been obtained.	HQM
	13	12 noon	Parade. 2nd Cav. Cav. Fd. Sta. 19. Remounts 18.	
	14		The usual morning Co: Parade. Con. a. n. s. Fd. Ced army & mother.	
			Capt BREWER & DETONARD due from England. Reinforcement presumably to terminate journey.	
		11 a.m.	ADMS inspected a large number of "unfit" in orderly room.	
		12 noon	ADM. 19. 2nd Cav. Cav. Fd. Sta. 12. 2nd Ind. B. Remounts.	
		2 pm	Some men of the unit rejected as unfit for Service campaigns.	
			7th Cav. Cav. Fd. Sta. -	
	15	9 a.m.	Capt BREWER and DETONARD reported on return from leave. Reports of cancelling of boat sailing. Lt. O. BOULTON A.S.C. joined the unit as Transport Officer.	
		12 both	ADM. 1 off. & 5. 2nd Cav. Cav. Fd. Sta. 1 & 6. 2nd Ind S. Remounts 9.	
		12 Mid	Show. had fallen in the night. Horse mornings — but later turf & chard yard was cold.	
			Received orders regarding motor amb. Waggons to follow Bde of Both Brigs. to their new quarters. Arranged this with the ASC so & Sergt CRAIG. No details given on more movement.	
			Ahead.	
	16	12 noon	Prog. Ko. was made. In signallers many of the unit with packs. Section Officers were at work packing their section equipment. 2 Inf. 1 morning 23.	
			ADM. 20. 2nd Cav. Cav. Fd. Sta. 5. 2nd Ind S. 4.	
			Mr T.S.R. BOYD reported on return from leave.	

Army Form C. 2118

WAR DIARY
or
INTELLIGENCE SUMMARY
(Erase heading not required.)

Instructions regarding War Diaries and Intelligence Summaries are contained in F.S. Regs., Part II. and the Staff Manual respectively. Title Pages will be prepared in manuscript.

Place	Date	Hour	Summary of Events and Information	Remarks and references to Appendices
FLOY	Nov 17	9 a.m.	An unpleasant occurrence came to light — In a suit fit of barbarous Capt; KREITTMAYER who had been in Amiens the previous night was brought a prisoner back to his billet but introduced him to the M.O. next morning. He was placed under arrest — In arresting Capt Capt DESMOND KLEMENT SMITH was assaulted — Seemed to be highly probable that the M.O. must be a trial by Court Martial.	
		12 noon	Adm 14 — To CCS 33. Cas 4 — Remg. 0 — The large number of evacuations over the subject of discussion with the ADMS. The M.O.S. maintained that each case was decided on its merits & that there was no intention of cases but the hopeless — ADMS came over to take a summary of evidence in connection with the KREITTMAYER case — Adm 9 — To CCS 9 — Remg 0 —	
	18	11 a.m.	News from the Balkans had most interesting — No figures seem to be made of the condition of the Serbians, &c — & no figures seem to be made of the participation of Greece on the side of the Central Powers —	
		12 noon	Considerable progress made in acquiring mules to transport when going — Adm 6 — Evac 3 Remg 3	
	9	12 noon	Weather remains anniably wet & raw — Packs are now provided for all men (RAMC) of the unit. Ambulances with the unit A raid was frequent.	

1875 Wt. W593/826 1,000,000 4/15 J.B.C. & A. A.D.S.S./Forms/C.2118.

Army Form C. 2118

WAR DIARY
or
INTELLIGENCE SUMMARY
(Erase heading not required.)

Instructions regarding War Diaries and Intelligence Summaries are contained in F.S. Regs., Part II. and the Staff Manual respectively. Title Pages will be prepared in manuscript.

Place	Date	Hour	Summary of Events and Information	Remarks and references to Appendices
FLY	Mar 20	10.30	Divine Service was held in the Village.	A.A.M
		12 noon	Adm:tted 5 – 2d Cav: Cly Sta: 3 – 2o Inf: 1 – Remains 4 –	
	21	9.30am	Evacno 3 – whole transport showed marked fatigue –	
		12 noon	Adm: 1 off. +13 – 2d Cav: Cly Sta: 1 off + 3 – 2o Inf: 4 – Remg: 13 –	
	22	11 a.m	BRAMS inspected motor ambts and "A" Car for evacuation of sick –	
		12 noon	Adm: 1 off +7 – 2d Cav: Cly Sta: 1 off +8. 2o Inf: 1 – Remg: 8.	
		2 pm	Received orders that Brms 6 wkld be moved railhead on 24th – being all animals but this waggons – also that 1/C A. Boyd was to be attached to R.E.
	23	10 a.m	Capt Hg WEIR was to join this unit – In accordance with finise orders 1/C BOYD was struck off strength on proceeds to-day with R.E. Capt H.W. WEIR was taken on strength attached to section –	
		12 noon	Packing has carried out with exception of section commanders – Adm: 1 office +7. 2d Cav. Cly Sta: 1 off +46 – 2o Inf: 3. Remains 4 – later Box Brains were also evacuated – Capt DEVONALD was detached for tempory duty with transport & details of R.I.Regt who were to follow at a later date – News was received of strong action of the Allies – Calculated to distinguish the retreat of Greeces on the side of the other –	
	24	10 a.m	2d Amb. left FLUY under command of Major STURROCK for LONGUEAU – the O.C. being at BOVELLIS on duty. Motor busses assisted march + 2d Amb reached LONGUEAU at 3pm. Wagons follows	

Army Form C. 2118

WAR DIARY
or
INTELLIGENCE SUMMARY
(Erase heading not required.)

Instructions regarding War Diaries and Intelligence Summaries are contained in F.S. Regs, Part II. and the Staff Manual respectively. Title Pages will be prepared in manuscript.

Place	Date	Hour	Summary of Events and Information	Remarks and references to Appendices
	24/11		1 hour later Transport Officer and A.S.C. personnel, all animals, and 10 ambulance wagons left behind. G.S. + limber wagons with 1 Maltese Cart (forge) and 1 Chaplains cart entrained. Personnel consists of 8 medical Officers, 1 Quarter 2 Chaplains and 173 other ranks. Sergt Major ARGENT was withdrawn to general depot at LONGUEAU.	AGGM
		5.20 pm	Train started and travelled pleasantly to destination. Food was well distributed. Tea could be obtained at the HALTES REPAS. There are three of these:— 1. MONTEREAU reached 6.40 a.m. Nov. 25th. 2. MACON " 10.15 pm " 3. PIERRELATTE " 8.30 a.m. Nov. 26th.	
	26th	4 pm	Reached MARSEILLES. Proceeded to embark on S.S. SATURNIA. Officers + men were housed for night, + all 2 wheeled vehicles put on board.	
	27th	10.30 am	2 G.S. wagons put on board. 4 are left behind under Capt. + 3 men to follow by later boat. By orders of A.D.M.S. 27th Division detailed Capts. BOYD and WIER to remain behind and act as M.O.'s to transports of 27th Division which were without M.O.'s	
		3 pm	Life belt parade for all N.C.O.'s + men. No movement took place during remainder of day or night.	
	28th	9 am	Divine Service.	

WAR DIARY or INTELLIGENCE SUMMARY

Army Form C. 2118

Place	Date	Hour	Summary of Events and Information	Remarks and references to Appendices
	28th	11.45am	Tugs came alongside and drew us out. By noon we were nearly free of the harbour. Sea smooth. Wind has gone round to E. remained cold. No letters reached us before sailing. Promotions carried out to fill vacancies. Cpl. Harris & Hodge to be acting Sergts. Sergt. Southam & Copblean absorbed into establishment. Qm. S. FREKMAN to be S.I. and acting S.M., S.S. MILDENHALL became Qmd. Sergts Morley & Lutherland became Staff Sergts, vice posts to B+C sections respectively. L/Cpl Weedon to be acting Corpl.	Algor
		4pm	Made TOULON Harbour, received by tugs. Remained till
		11pm	Slowed out to sea steered E.N.E.
	29th	8am	ALPS MARITIMES could be seen in distance on Port bow. We were apparently heading for a point not far south of GENOA. There was a slight return in a large number of N.CO. men were prostrated with seasickness.
		1pm	CORSICA appeared on starboard bow. We steered for the N. of the island & proceeded in a southerly direction between CORSICA & ELBA. Boats & rafts were apportioned to various units.
	30th	8am	Very much warmer. Boat was now about 25 miles E. of SARDINIAN coast on a level with NAPLES. A FRENCH destroyer appeared, spoke to us & accompanied us for some hours. MARCONI news states that SICILY was literally besieged by German submarines

WAR DIARY
or
INTELLIGENCE SUMMARY

(Erase heading not required.)

Army Form C. 2118

Place	Date	Hour	Summary of Events and Information	Remarks and references to Appendices
	30th	8am	Crew told off to boats under Capt. GRIFFITH and Major STURROCK. Later a list of Rafts Squads was made out. 2 boats & 6 rafts were allotted to the Fd. Amb	AGM
		12 noon	About this time we began to take a zigzag course. The destroyers returned to us & about 3 pm we fell in with other transports & a column was formed.	
		4pm	"Alarm" for practice.	

WO95/2259/4

27TH DIVISION
MEDICAL

NO. 7 SANITARY SECTION
DEC 1915

27

Sanitary Sect.
Dec X
Vol I

15

Dec 1915 Summarised but not copied

27th Div
F/260/1

7 San. Sect.

Army Form C. 2118.

WAR DIARY
INTELLIGENCE SUMMARY.
(Erase heading not required)

No 9 Sanitary Section (Indian Attached) 27th Divison.

Instructions regarding War Diaries and Intelligence Summaries are contained in F. S. Regs., Part II. and the Staff Manual respectively. Title pages will be prepared in manuscript.

Place	Date	Hour	Summary of Events and Information	Remarks and references to Appendices
BOVELLES FRANCE	1915 1 Dec	—	Entrained at Longneau (marched from Bouvelles).	
"	2 "	—	In train.	
"	3 "	—	Arrived at Marseilles about 9 pm marched to camp Parc Borely.	
MARSEILLES FRANCE.	4 " to 3rd	—	In camp Parc Borely. Party of men from section employed daily on general sanitary fatigue, clearing latrine buckets, assisting at manure burning. General refitting with equipment, clothing & tools, overhaul of harness for mules, repair of wagon and exercise mule team. About Dec 13th a private of the 2nd Batt R.I.R. (attached) was taken to hospital and died of pneumonia.	

G White
Capt to R.A.M.C.(T)

www.ingramcontent.com/pod-product-compliance
Lightning Source LLC
Chambersburg PA
CBHW081431160426
43193CB00013B/2250